Roti

40 Classic Indian Breads & Sides

Nandita Godbole

Forewords
Raghavan Iyer
Ken Albala

Second Edition | Turmeric Press

Best wishes.
[illegible]
2020.

Copyright Page

For all permission requests, contact the author and artist directly:
Nandita Godbole
www.currycravingskitchen.com / www.currycravings.com
currycravings@gmail.com

Text, Food Styling, Graphic Design & Art: Nandita Godbole
Forewords: Raghavan Iyer & Ken Albala
Editor (Print & eBook): R. Umashankar

Publisher's Cataloging-in-Publication Data
Godbole, Nandita
Roti: 40 Classic Indian Breads & Sides
ISBN: 978-1-940957-18-0

1. Indian. 2. Bread 3. Recipes 4. Cooking. 5. Spices

Second Edition. Limited Release
Turmeric Press

Dedicated to my mother for the many hours she spent
teaching me to roll a perfect rotli,
and to my father, who enjoyed every single one I made.

Contents

Sides: Chutneys, Raitas & More (continued)

Foreword

Chef Raghavan Iyer, CCP

Rotis, a generic representation of breads, are anything but mundane. Rotis and Indian food go together like a horse and carriage, yes, a new analogy to an old well-heeled song. We use them as eating utensils at every meal, breaking them apart into bite-size morsels with the forefingers of your right hand (an etiquette in a culture where EVERYTHING is done with hands – the left reserved for hygiene), wrapping them around delectable curries, succulent stir-fries, and potent condiments.

So, to have Nandita's roti recipes that span the versatility of India's regional fare, is a boon. Every recipe is meticulously laid out, a series of pictures dot its steps, a finished product that begs you to make your own stack. Many of them appear easy to make, and they are, once you master the techniques, because, like their European counterparts, it's all in the hands, the feel, the appropriate amount of moisture, the right cooking method, and yes, even the shaped thickness.

In addition to everyday fare like the ubiquitous roti, you will find some gems that showcase breads from her childhood, Puran Poli, sweetened pigeon peas stuffed into flaky-tender whole wheat breads and griddle cooked, and the way I savor it, with mounds of warm clarified butter. Or Methi theplas, Gujarat's addictive fenugreek-studded flatbreads with ginger. Some batter-based recipes round out the mélange, every recipe an inviting trip down memory lane.

Oh and don't forget to make those amazing sides of chutneys and raitas that complement every type of bread in this book. Rotis-r-us!

Raghavan Iyer
Author.Consultant.Spokesperson.

Foreword
Prof. Ken Albala, University of the Pacific

Like me, you can probably remember the first time you tasted that slightly crisp yet chewy, airy wonder redolent of butter, offered at the start of a classic Indian meal. It awakens the senses, stimulates the appetite and opens the imagination for the meal to come. There is nothing like it in the Western canon and no technique there that will help you achieve that unforgettable texture and aroma. Fortunately, there is now a book to explain it all for the home cook.

Despite the intense interest in baking nowadays, few people have the knowledge or skills to tackle the wide array of Indian breads that are essential to Indian cuisine. Come to think of it, these breads would also make an excellent addition to any cook's repertoire and in any context. This marvelous book goes way beyond the familiar naan and includes delicate paratha, fermented dosa, fried bhatura, stuffed and flavored breads, and so many exquisite sounding recipes that I dare anyone to resist running straight to the kitchen after reading it.

The instructions are clear and concise, beautifully illustrated with photographs of various steps. There are descriptions of the ingredients, the necessary tools and techniques as well as a whole array of condiments and sides to accompany the breads. Even the seasoned cook will make many new discoveries here. Of course the breads themselves draw from a tradition that is thousands of years old. They have been perfected by generations of hands plying the dough into perfect form after centuries of experience. All this has been condensed into a single accessible source that will entice both the neophyte and the veteran baker.

I dare say this book will take a place of pride on the cook's shelf next to classics by Julie Sahni and Madhur Jaffrey. That's exactly where it will go in my library.

Ken Albala
Author, Professor of History & Food Writer
University of the Pacific

Roti

40 Classic Indian Breads & Sides

Introduction to Indian Breads

Indian breads are a traditional, customary part of an Indian meal, and most Indian meals feel incomplete without them. They often facilitate the enjoyment of freshly cooked vegetable entrees, become the carriers of rich sauces and stews and offer a neutral base to polish off the spices and seasonings off the plate into the mouth without much effort.

A quick sampling of Indian breads will show that there are many ways to categorize them: by types of flour, size, seasonings, leavening, dough versus batter, and even cooking method. Whole grain ingredients like wheat, rice, buckwheat, millets, corn and others, or even a combination of several whole grain flours are popular. They vary in shape, size, flavor and method of preparation. They can be thin or fat, plain or seasoned, laminated or layered, stuffed or unstuffed, sweet or savory, as also unleavened or leavened. Some are bound with water, others with milk, weak buttermilk (yogurt based), plain yogurt, or other ingredients. The fats incorporated during binding can be oil, butter, or ghee to sometimes, yogurt. Cooking methods can vary based on the dough. While most are stove top preparations, both griddle-fried or deep-fried, others are baked in a tandoor or oven, or even cooked directly on an open flame. Regional variations are reflected in not only the preferred ingredients but also in their name. What is called roti in Northern India is called pol'y in Western India. Puran poli (or Pooran Poli), synonymous with a stuffed sweet flatbread in most of the country is also known as mevdi in some parts of Western India. While Southern India is famous for its crunchy dosas, a fermented, ground rice and lentil batter-based bread, the cuisine of Northern India is known for its delectable stuffed parathas.

All these differences suggest only one thing –that this food group holds enough diversity and interest to captivate both cooking enthusiasts and diners alike.

Common Raw Materials: Flour

Indian breads use a variety of base ingredients to make into flour. The cuisine has adapted not only rice and wheat, but also other grains like millets, starches and even lentils and legumes, in both dough and batter forms. Each of these differ in taste, texture and gluten content, and offer a variety of diet-friendly options. Unlike vegetables that lend themselves to a variety of preparation methods with ease, the basic ingredients of the bread determines the corresponding cooking method. For instance, although dry flour may be used for dusting and rolling a griddle-fried bread preparation, if the same dough is used to make poori which is deep-fried, then the dough is rolled using oil! In short, there are many kinds of Indian breads, and to understand the differences and therefore the breads themselves, one must understand their ingredients and preparation techniques. Here are a few of the more commonly used ingredients to make flour or batter.

- **Wheat**
  Unlike the rest of the world, in the United States, commercially available bread flour or whole wheat flour is made from hard red wheat berries. Red wheat berries do not yield a flour suitable for making rotis or parathas on account of its high protein content. It is also a heavier flour that requires leavening agents to lift it, making it more suitable for baking. Flour made from these berries are not suited to making Indian rotis, because most of them are unleavened. The most common wheat berry for flour in India is the durum wheat berry. These berries are light golden in color and plump, and the flour is a warm yellowish tan pillowy powder. It makes for soft rotis and parathas, and is ideal for preparations that do not use any form of leavening. Coarsely ground durum wheat berries first yield a version of cracked wheat, followed by increasingly finer grades of semolina, with wheat flour being the finest grade of flour.

- **Rice**
  Rice flour is a popular addition to pantries in India and is frequently used to prepare a fat, tortilla-like flatbread known as bhakri. The flour is silky and smooth and yields a soft dough that can become dry and brittle very quickly during the cooking process. Converting rice flour to a pliable dough is an easy process and the resulting flatbread has a rustic quality to it. Different varieties of rice are popular for making rice flour. Polished Basmati rice makes for a bright white flour and yields a drier bhakri whereas flour made from unpolished red rice or rice varieties yield a moister bhakri. Rice bhakris typically don't perform very well when reheated and are less convenient to make in modern kitchens. However, for the occasional indulgence, these are definitely worthy of one's culinary repertoire.

- **Bajra & Jowar**
  Pearl millet and sorghum are known as bajra and jowar respectively in India. These two grains are a staple in much of rural India. They are more nutritious than ordinary wheat flour and are often considered a "farmers' bread." Pearl millet yields a sage green flour while sorghum flour is pale yellowish in color.

- **Ragi**
  Ragi or finger millet is slightly smaller in size and shape compared to red quinoa grains. High in fiber, nutrition, gluten-free, and easy to digest, this grain is often a preferred addition to the diets of people recovering from illnesses. The grain yields a reddish-brown flour and since it lacks gluten needs binding agents to convert into a dough.

- **Corn**
  Corn flour is popular in northern India, and makes 'makkey-ki-roti', or roti made from corn. Similar to the corn tortillas of Mexico, corn rotis are drier and coarse when compared to other kinds of roti's. Some recipes call for including a portion of wheat flour to make the dough more pliable. Served alongside a dollop of churned butter, these rotis are popular in rustic meals.

- **Chickpeas & Chickpea flour**
  Chickpeas, also known as garbanzo beans are the key ingredient in many gluten-free flatbreads and batter-based breads. Dried skinless split chickpeas are soaked and ground for savory pancakes like adai. Chickpea flour, more commonly known as besan, is protein rich and nutritious. Much like ragi flour it too lacks gluten and is better suited for batter-based preparations. Most often, chickpea flour is used to make besan poora, a batter-based griddle fried savory pancake.

- **Buckwheat**
  A less common flour in urban areas, buckwheat is similar to any other low gluten flour and is great for batter-based preparations or when making bhakri.

- **Mung beans**
  Dried green mung beans when ground yield a sage green colored flour. It is very high in nutrition and gluten-free. In most households, whole skinned mung beans are soaked overnight and ground into a wet pasty batter, blended with other grain-based batters such as soaked and ground rice. The resulting batter base makes dosas or crepe-like preparations. Popular in southern India, paserattu is made from soaked and ground mung beans combined with freshly grated coconut, or coconut milk, spices and other flavorings for a hearty savory dosa. Split yellow mung beans can also be used in the same manner to yield a similar dosa or paserattu.

- **Combination / blends**
  Some recipes call for a combination of one or more grains or flours, to balance out the low gluten content of another ingredient. Popular additives include tapioca or sago pearls or flour, or whole or skinless split masoor or red lentils. In many such recipes, fermentation times and binding agents will vary from the norm.

Other Raw Materials

- **Binding agents & fats**
  Different recipes require different binding agents to convert dry flour to dough or batter. Some basic doughs are formed with regular water, others require warm water, Greek yogurt, chaas or Indian buttermilk. The addition of fats will depend on the recipe with most requiring a small dash of oil. Each binding agent is carefully chosen so as to enhance the flavors in the flour and any seasonings used, withstand the cooking method, and boost the texture of the finished bread.

- **Rising agents**
  Part of the cooking process is to understand how the dough will react to the heat and how quickly it will cook. Wheat breads that are griddle-cooked seldom require a rising agent. Some recipes call for baking powder, baking soda or yeast. Although this book does not include any such recipes some batter-based preparations call for beer that does the work of a binding agent and rising agent. Both, the cooking method and the type of flour used, will determine which rising agent is preferred.

  Fermented batters depend on the light and airy texture created in the fermenting process to give the batter some body and bounce. Naturally occurring fermentation is popular in many dishes across Southern India. In some recipes, neera (a palm sap that converts into toddy during fermentation) is added to hasten the fermentation process and sweeten the batter as it ferments. In other recipes, a teaspoon of homemade yogurt does the trick.

- **Seasonings & fillings**
  Sometimes during the binding process, at other times incorporated later, seasonings and fillings give each bread variety its own flavor and flair. From trying to extend the flavors of seasonal produce to creating a hearty one-dish meal, making a dessert, or incorporating leftovers, there are many options to take a basic dough and convert into something else. This book also includes a few different breads that serve as desserts.

Doughs, Batters & Processes

At the very least, there are two distinctly different results of combining a flour with a binding agent and possibly a rising agent: either one gets a dough or a batter. Both perform differently in the cooking process.

The simplest dough is for roti. It starts with four basic ingredients: flour, water, salt and a little oil. Although one would think that rolling a roti is the logical next step after the dough is made, that does not always apply to all dough-based breads. Across India there are a few different methods – beyond the common practice. Some cooks and recipes call for rolling the dough right away, others call for resting for a few minutes. Wheat-based doughs that do not include leavening or rising agents also benefit from extended kneading to activate the gluten. Another age-old and effective way to maximize benefit from wheat dough for roti is still popular in rural Maharashtra, called "kanik-bhijawne," a phrase that literally translates into "soaking the grain." In this method, flour, water and salt are first combined in a shallow pan into a dough. This dough is then patted down, sprinkled with water and allowed to rest for 10-20 minutes. The rested dough is then kneaded, incorporating the water into the dough. In the last few seconds, a light bit of oil is kneaded in to prevent the dough from drying. This also fortifies the elasticity of the dough. Like the resting phase or proofing phase when making yeast-based breads, this process also lightens and alters the texture of the resulting bread. The second kneading also activates the gluten, makes for a softer roti and such rotis are easier to digest, making them even more nutritious.

Breads made from gluten-free flours are typically called "bhakri." Gluten-free flours like jowar, bajra or rice flour are typically bound with warm water so that the resulting dough is pliable. However, the resulting dough is tender and must be shaped carefully. The old-fashioned way of working this kind of dough is by flattening out the dough by hand, between one's palms and then gently but quickly working to make a large, evenly thick bhakri. In modern kitchens, such dough can be rolled with a very light hand, for an even thickness. The cooking method for such bhakri varies slightly as compared to others. Most breads made from gluten-free flours are always griddle fried or cooked directly over the flame, never deep fried.

Batter-based breads include dosas, ghavan, crepes and such. Some require fermentation, others don't. Most are cooked on a non-stick pan or griddle.

Common Tools

As you become familiar with the technique of rolling Indian breads, you will find that the delicacy of Indian breads comes from a combination of factors, key being the tools used to roll the dough. Gentle and light rolling of the dough on a proper rolling surface traps and creates air pockets in the dough, and when combined with the right cooking method, goes on to create light and delicate layers in the roti or paratha. Most Indian breads require a few basic tools to get started. Here a few things you will need.

- **Tortilla Press, Pasta Mill Or Tapered Rolling Pin?**
  To understand what kind of tools are best suited, one must first understand the structure of the roti. Roti involves stretching the dough into thin sheets, much like pizza dough. These thinly stretched sheets of dough rely on the proper treatment of raw materials to create soft and supple flatbreads. The flour provides the structure, any gluten helps with the elasticity, the binding liquid steams the dough as it evaporates during the cooking process and creates light air pockets whereas the added fats strengthen elasticity and make the finished rotis soft. A light basting of ghee is recommended to the finished roti to keep it from drying out. Although the mark of a skilled roti maker may be their perfectly shaped rotis, shape is largely inconsequential in its final result -- its texture and taste is.

  Most amateurs try to outsmart the seemingly complicated roti rolling method at least once because it appears to be a timesaver by using the pie crust method. Here, amateurs try to roll out the dough into one large sheet using whatever cylindrical tool they can find, and then trim out circular rounds. Although this may appear to work in theory, it yields cracker-like diskettes because doing so has completely altered dough. First, the weight of the rolling tool pushes out the dough differently. Second, rolling out the dough into a large sheet dries out what little moisture is needed to help the dough cook over a hot griddle. Third, cutting the dough creates a sharp seam that trims any air pockets that would have otherwise been created during the correct rolling of the dough. These trimmed edges are typically the first to brown or crisp, and give a false perception that the roti is cooked enough. Lastly, re-using the trimmed dough to make more rotis requires additional dry flour, and changes the pliability of the dough. This overworks any remaining gluten into tough strands that do not perform well when heated. All in all, although commercial operations produce roti's for retail in this manner, the pie crust method does not work for a roti made at home.

Other methods that don't offer optimal results include bypassing the rolling by using a tortilla press or a pasta extruder. Neither devices are ideal tools because they exert uneven pressure on the dough. The dough is either uniformly thick (pasta extruder) or stretched more in one direction (tortilla press). Using these devices also requires altering the dough recipe to include a higher proportion of oil to retain elasticity. Tortilla presses however work for making pooris, because pooris are smaller and are deep-fired and therefore each diskette becomes immersed in the hot oil all at once.

Mechanized roti making gadgets become an expensive addition to the casual kitchen, especially one that that struggles for counter space. These also require more time to produce a batch large enough to feed a family.

The delicate roti making process was long perfected in India with the traditional Indian tapered rolling pins, an essential in kitchens that cook Indian food. The tapered rolling pin is called by different names depending on the region of India - belan in Hindi, velan in Gujarati or latna in Marathi. They are easily available in ethnic markets along with other roti making tools. Belan is the preferred tool when making rotis and similar Indian breads.

A belan is a long dowel-like tool, at least a foot long with a center no more than two inches in diameter, with graduated tapered ends ranging from half inch to a quarter inch in diameter. They are most often made of wood, although some are available in metal as well. The slender design of the belan is widest in the center and has gradually tapered ends, allowing the chef to roll the dough smoothly and evenly without creating folds, bumps or tears. It needs only light pressure of one's finger tips and palm to stretch the dough. The ends keep one's fingers away from the surface, and prevents accidental dragging or pulling of the dough. In some ways, it also offers a "check" for size. To make thin rotis, rolling is completed in large strokes, a series of sweeping and continuous motions rather than short bursts. To visualize it, think of the uncooked roti in the shape of the traditional belan in cross-section.

A pastry rolling pin (French or other), a pie pastry rolling pin with rollers, or those made of marble do not work as well for rolling out the dough for Indian breads because they put too much pressure on the dough, not letting it remain light and airy. These are heavier to use and become even more impractical when making a large batch of light and delicate rotis. Although the Turkish oklava creates very thin sheets of dough, it is not a good alternate tool for making roti. Textured rolling pins are not suitable either.

A well-made roti is soft, cooked all the way through evenly, has no crisp edges and retains its freshly made "sweetness" several hours after it is cooked. Bypassing the method by using unsuitable rolling equipment, or incorrect rolling methods will never yield satisfactory results.

- **Rolling Platform**

  Skilled roti makers use anything from a polished clean kitchen counter to an upturned flat-bottom cake pan secured in place over a thick kitchen towel to roll their roti. However, this requires a certain confidence that amateurs must work towards.

  The rolling surface for making Indian breads is typically a raised platform called chakla in Hindi, o'ras'u in Gujarati or pol'pat in Marathi. Platforms are most often made from marble or wood. Metal platforms are also available. These are a personal preference. For an early learner, the smooth metallic surface offers little resistance to the rolling process and the dough slides around when least expected. Tiny sturdy legs raise the platform 2-3 inches above the main cooking counter. This allows you to roll the dough without hitting or dragging your fingers on the kitchen counter. The rolling pin and platform are often sold as sets, but if looking to replace only one of them, be sure that the platform is smaller than the rolling pin.

- **Cooking Utensils: Pots & Pans**

  Most non-stick crepe pans will serve well as a griddle for making Indian breads. Earthen griddles are great for making rustic bhakris but must be worked with carefully once they heat up. In the absence of a tandoor, ceramic pizza stones work great in the oven to replicate the taste of a freshly made naan. Fried breads like pooris and bhaturas require the use of a deep fryer. Air fryers are not recommended. A pair of flat-nosed tongs will help with making phulkas, a flat spatula is useful when making griddle fried breads, and a spider helps with making pooris and fried breads. A mesh basket is useful while cooling freshly made flatbreads and pooris.

- **Cooking Devices: Stoves, Grills, Ovens**

  Both electric and natural gas stoves will work for making most Indian flatbreads. However, for making flame-cooked phulkas/fulkas a natural gas stove is preferable. Its puffed form gives this bread its name – the word "fulka" suggesting light, puffed or delicate. This puffed quality can be mimicked on an electric stove but it misses the slightly smoky sweetness that comes from cooking over an open-flame. Induction stoves are not ideal for making phulka roti's but suffice for most other preparations.

  Naans are traditionally best made in a tandoor oven, but even home-tandoors for a backyard are not a very practical household addition for everyday kitchens. Many updated grills with a ceramic interior can be adapted for the purpose of making naan. A working oven that has a broiler, when paired with a ceramic pizza stone also yields excellent results.

Rolling & Cooking Techniques

Different kinds of Indian breads can require slightly different techniques. Mastering the technique for one may take a few tries but once you perfect the technique for one, you can adapt it easily to other recipes.

Finishing Touches

Most breads are finished, by default, with a light basting of butter or ghee. This keeps it moist and pliable. Sprinklings of garnishes such as chopped cilantro or toasted seeds or nuts are more common in the hospitality industry than are at home.

Storing & Reheating Bread

Due to the high protein content in most Indian breads, they do not store well at room temperature for more than a day. To extend the life of the rotis and such, once cooled, place them in an airtight container in the refrigerator. Reheat on a warm griddle with a light basting of butter or ghee, or within a foil packet in a warm oven set to 170-180°F for 5 minutes or until just warmed. Do not microwave as they will get chewy at first and then become dry and brittle.

Breaking Bread

It is very common for those not familiar with traditional eating practices to treat Indian breads in the same way as they would a tortilla or a slice of bread, where the diner tears the bread with two hands into bite sized pieces and then uses their left hand to eat a bite of bread and their right hand to scoop up a piece of the entrée with a spoon, or create a roll-up, and chow down alternate bites of the bread and the entrée. Roti is never eaten in the same morsel as rice. Although it may feel easy to do, traditional homes are likely to frown upon such dinner table manners for various reasons. Though initially it will feel a little clumsy, just like the first time one may have used chopsticks, once a diner gets the simplicity of the motion, it makes for effortless, single hand eating.

- **How To Break Bread**
  Place the roti or bread flat on the plate. Using one's right hand, grab an edge between the thumb, forefinger and middle finger and place remaining fingers below. Using a tearing motion, pull the bread slightly towards yourself, using only the thumb, your ring finger and if needed your pinkie. You should now have a bite-sized piece of bread in your hand, ready to eat. Fold it over a portion of the entrée or dip into any sauce-based food on your plate.

In This Book

To simplify this book, breads are organized into a few broad sections.

- **Griddle-fried Unseasoned Breads**
  This basic section includes everyday breads that are unleavened and unseasoned, cooked specifically using a griddle.
- **Griddle-fried Seasoned Breads**
  These griddle fried breads incorporate seasonings and spices directly into the flour.
- **Griddle-fried Stuffed Breads**
  These griddle fried breads require a base dough and a "stuffing."
- **Fried Breads**
  This category includes both unleavened and leavened breads, that may or may not be seasoned with spices.
- **Freehand Breads**
  These breads use a variety of tools, have a rising agent and are adaptable to other preparations.
- **Batter-based Breads**
  These breads include both fermented and unfermented preparations.
- **Sides: Chutneys, Raitas & More**
  This section includes both savory and sweet pairings for breads.

Nearly all sections include both savory and sweet preparations. Rolling and cooking techniques applicable across several recipes are illustrated via a single set that depicts the process through step-by-step photographs.

The book includes forty classic breads and nearly two dozen sides are consumed every day all across India. The selections included here only scratch the surface of hundreds of regional varieties but offer a good place to start learning how to incorporate whole grains into ones diet for a healthier lifestyle. Enjoy.

Poori served with freshly extracted ripe mango pulp is a summertime favorite.

Griddle-fried Unseasoned Breads

Griddle-fried breads are easy to make, require less preparation than other breads and compliment most Indian main courses. These are typically used for daily meals. Most are savory, although some regional varieties may be sweet as well. There are two broad kinds: wheat-based griddle-fried varieties and non-wheat based griddle-fried varieties.

Wheat-Based Basic Breads: Roti & Others

Most everyday breads are made from wheat flour. As simple unleavened breads, parathas, roti/fulka/phulkas, and pol'ya are considered basic or everyday breads in an Indian meal. They use durum wheat flour, salt, water and a dash of oil to bind. The dough comes together quickly and requires little or no coaxing. Overworking the dough can make the rotis and parathas tough.

Each recipe includes dough making instructions that may vary slightly. Upon rolling the dough out, as one of the recipes will show, differences in cooking methods can yield different types of breads as listed below:

(a) griddle-fried, basted with ghee to make paratha,

(b) first griddle-cooked and then flame-roasted to make roti/fulka/phulka,

(c) rolled once, layered with a basting of ghee in between, rolled again and griddle fried using ghee to make a layered paratha or poly'a.

Non-Wheat Based Breads: Bhakri & Other Gluten-free Basic Breads

The word "bhakri" suggests the use of low gluten flours such as rice, millets, sorghum, amaranth, buckwheat and others. Usually made from a single type of grain flour, and sometimes two or more, bhakris are typically thicker and have a dry texture and can have low or no gluten at all, e.g. rice flour. The bhakri dough is most often bound with warm water, salt, and ghee. Traditionally, the dough is flattened by hand with a dusting of dry flour, first griddle-roasted and then flame-roasted. Traditionally made bhakris are unfortunately becoming a lost art, and most people are not comfortable roasting over an open flame. Bhakris can still be made in modern kitchens by rolling out the dough using a rolling pin and then cooked on a griddle.

STEPS: WHOLE WHEAT DOUGH FOR ROTI, PARATHA, STUFFED PARATHA ETC

1. Assemble ingredients: flour, water, salt & oil.

2. Add salt.

3. Add half the water.

4. Reserve other half of the water for later.

5. Mix in the water with the flour.

6. Knead in all the dry flour.

7. Mix in the remaining water and knead again.

8. Add the oil and knead it in.

9. Finished ball of dough.

10. Divide the dough into equal portions.

Steps: How to roll roti, fulka, paratha, etc

1. Arrange workspace.

2. Dredge a single dough ball in dry flour.

3. Dust off excess dry flour.

4. Use pinched hold & light pressure.

5. Continue rolling, use 'pinched' hold.

6. Dust with dry flour as needed.

7. Spread flour, flip, continue rolling.

8. Finished, rolled uncooked roti.

Paratha

Griddle-fried Whole Wheat Bread

Makes: Eight 2-piece servings
Prep Time: 10 minutes
Cook Time: Less than 30 minutes

A staple of most Indian meals, paratha is a more festival-appropriate version of whole wheat roti. This is a simple introduction to a version of roti and a suitable place to start for a novice cook, as it takes some practice.

Ingredients

3 cups atta (stone-ground durum whole wheat flour), sifted, plus extra for dredging
1½ cup or more water for binding
Salt, to taste
½ tsp oil
2-5 tbsp ghee

Method: To Bind

Using a food processor fitted with an S-blade or in a large bowl, combine the flour with salt and enough water to make a firm dough. The dough should be firm but not hard, moist but not wet, and similar in consistency of modeling clay. Carefully knead the oil into the dough and cover with a clear wrap or lid until ready to roll.

Method: To Roll

Divide the dough into golf-ball-sized pieces. Using the palms of your hands, roll each piece into a smooth ball and lightly flatten to make 1″ diskettes. Keep these covered to avoid drying. Dredge only the diskette you are going to roll in the dry flour. Using a tapered rolling pin, gently roll out the dough using the pressure of your hands to make it move slightly and spin/rotate. Using light pressure, move the rolling pin along a small circular path as you roll back and forth will help the dough spin. Roll outwards but not over the edge. Dredge with dry flour as needed to avoid stickiness. Lightly dust off the finished uncooked paratha before placing on the griddle.

Method: To Cook

Heat a griddle or shallow nonstick pan on medium-high heat. When ready to place a paratha in the pan, turn it down to medium heat. The side that hits the pan first is the first side. Watch for the dough to bubble slightly and move it around in the pan to avoid hot spots. Turn the paratha over approximately a minute later. The first side should be lightly spotted but not have burnt spots. If this happens, reduce the heat. Repeat on the second side, and while the second side cooks, lightly baste the first side with ghee. Using a spatula, flip the paratha and baste the second side. Both sides should have ghee: cooked once without ghee and once with ghee. Remove from heat and cover with a paper towel or a colander to help the steam evaporate. Once they have come to room temperature, the parathas can be transferred to an appropriate storage container.

Paratha paired with a shrikhand that is topped with diced fresh mango

Chapati/Fulka Roti/Rotli

Flame-Cooked Puffed Whole Wheat Chapati

Makes: Eight 2-piece servings
Cook Time: 30 minutes

Called by many names this is an essential piece of a simple everyday Indian meal. The names chapati, roti, rotli are regional references to the same kind of bread. The term "fulka" is an adjective that reflects its fluffy nature, a result of direct flame cooking. Instead of the flame cooking, when cooked only on a griddle, the resulting bread is called a roti or chapati. The term "rotli" is specifically used in Gujarat to emphasize the smaller and delicate nature of this bread. The rolling technique perfected using a very light hand, makes these a rewarding preparation.

Ingredients

3 cups atta (stone-ground durum whole wheat flour), sifted, plus extra for dredging
1½ cup or more water for binding
Salt, to taste
½ tsp oil
2-5 tbsp ghee

Method: To Bind

Using a food processor fitted with an S-blade or in a large bowl, combine the flour with salt and enough water to make a firm dough. The dough should be firm but not hard, moist but not wet, and similar in consistency to modeling clay. Carefully knead the oil into the dough and cover with a clear wrap or lid until ready to roll. Divide the dough into golf ball-sized pieces. Using the palms of your hands, roll each piece into a smooth ball and lightly flatten to make 1" diskettes. Keep these covered to avoid drying.

Method: To Roll

Dredge only the diskette you are going to roll in the dry flour. Using a tapered rolling pin, gently roll out the dough using the pressure of your hands to make it move slightly and spin/rotate. Using light pressure on the pin and moving the rolling pin along a small circular path as you roll back and forth will help the dough spin. Roll outwards but not over the edge. Routinely dredge/dust with dry flour as needed to avoid stickiness. Lightly dust off the finished uncooked rotli. Each uncooked rotli should be the thickness of an uncooked lasagna sheet or slightly thinner.

Method: To Cook Directly On The Gas Flame

Heat a griddle or shallow nonstick pan on medium-high heat. When ready to place a rotli in the pan, turn it down to medium heat. The side that hits the pan first is the first side. Watch for the dough to bubble slightly and move it around in the pan to avoid hotspots. Turn the rotli over approximately a minute later. Increase the heat to medium high. The first side should be lightly spotted but not have dark spots. Repeat on the second side. Using a pair of tongs, directly transfer the partially cooked rotli, side one down, directly onto the flame of the burner. The rotli will begin to puff up. Pick it up with the tongs, flip it and set it down again, turning as you go. Do this on each side at least once. Remove from flame and pat down to help dissipate the steam. Lightly baste with ghee. Once they have come to room temperature, the rotlis can be transferred to an appropriate storage container.

Method: To Cook Only On The Griddle (suitable for both gas and electric stoves)

Heat a griddle or shallow nonstick pan on medium-high heat. When ready to place a flattened uncooked rotli in the pan, turn it down to medium-low heat. The side that hits the pan first is the first side. Watch for the uncooked rotli to bubble up slightly and move it around in the pan without flipping it over to avoid hotspots. Turn the rotli over approximately a minute later. Increase the heat to medium. The first side should be lightly spotted but not have dark spots. Repeat on the second side. Now flip the chapati over back to side one. Use a dry kitchen towel wad to very gently push the bubbles down and around on the griddle. This light pressure will move the trapped air between the two sides of dough. The rotli may puff up just a little. Flip after one minute, and repeat the same on the second side. Each side should be cooked once without being pushed down, and once being pushed down. Use a pair of tongs to transfer it from the griddle to your container. Pat down to help dissipate any steam. Lightly baste with ghee. Once they have come to room temperature, the finished rotli/roti/chapati can be transferred to an appropriate storage container.

1. Place rolled roti on warm non-stick griddle.

2. Cook on medium low until underside bubbles, the side touching the griddle is side #1.

3. Move it around once or twice, and flip it. Side #1 will be lightly spotted.

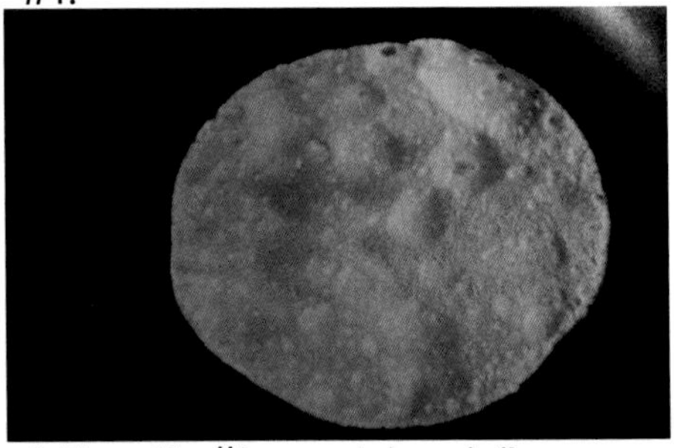

4. Allow side #2 to cook in a similar manner.

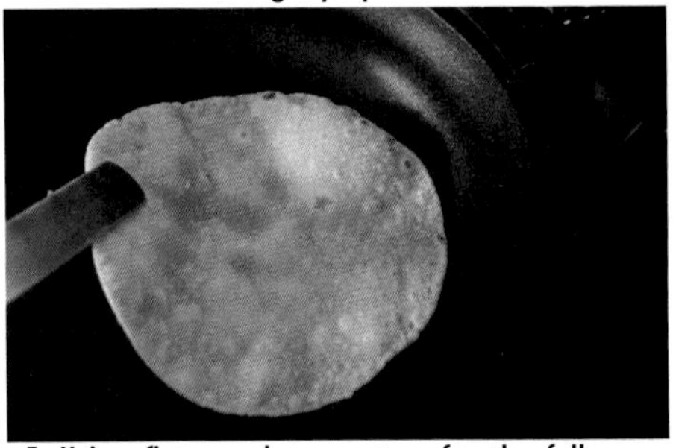

5. Using flat-nosed tongs, transfer the fulka onto the open flame.

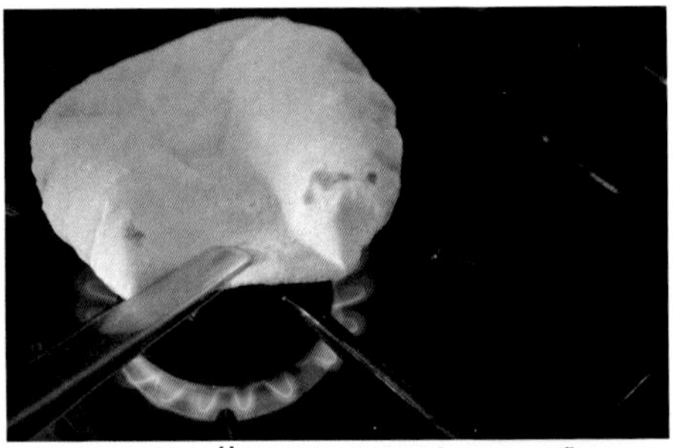

6. Place side #1 down onto the open flame.

7. Cook once on either side until fulka puffs up, 7-10 seconds on each side.

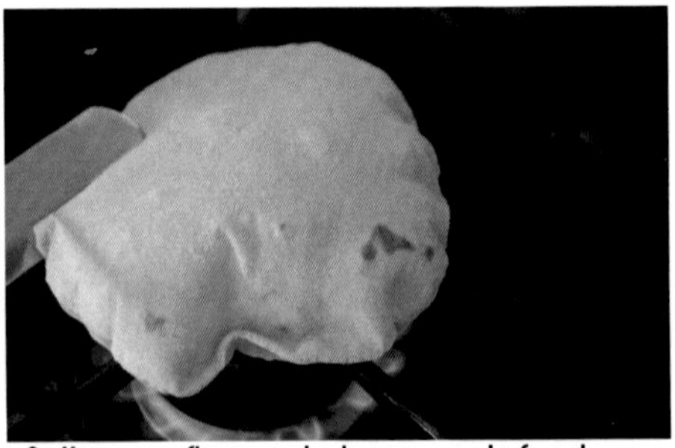

8. Keep on flame only long enough for the fulka to puff up, no more than twice on each side.

9. Remove from flame into a flat bottom colander.

10. Baste with melted ghee while still warm.

Ghadi-chya Pol'ya

Layered Paratha or Whole Wheat Griddle-fried Bread

Makes: Twelve to fifteen 8" pol'ya
Cook Time: 30-45 minutes

Typically popular along the upper west coast of India, these laminated breads are often requested at larger gatherings because they are fairly fail-proof and look as though it took hours to prepare. Each pol'y (plural: pol'ya) uses a generous application of ghee, once to layer them, and a second time for basting while griddle frying them.

Ingredients

3 cups atta (stone-ground durum whole wheat flour), sifted, plus extra for dredging
1½ cup or more water for binding
Salt, to taste
½ tsp oil
3-5 tbsp ghee, melted

Method: To Bind

Using a food processor fitted with an S-blade or in a large bowl, combine the flour with salt and enough water to make a firm dough. The dough should be firm but not hard, moist but not wet, and similar in consistency to modeling clay. Carefully knead the oil into the dough and cover with a clear wrap for 10 minutes and rest the dough until ready to roll. Divide the dough into golf-ball-sized pieces. Using the palms of your hands, roll each piece into a smooth ball and lightly flatten to make 1" diskettes. Keep these covered to avoid drying.

Method: To Roll

Dredge only the diskette you are going to roll in the dry flour. Using a tapered rolling pin, gently roll out the dough using the pressure of your hands to make it move slightly and spin/rotate. Moving the rolling pin along a small circular path, rolling outwards but not over the edge, roll until it is a four-inch disk. Baste a small amount of melted ghee on one side of the disk and fold the disk over itself, first into a half. Apply some ghee to the exposed half, and fold it over itself again into to a pie-wedge-shaped piece of folded dough. Dredge or lightly dust with dry flour to avoid stickiness. Very lightly repeat rolling out the folded dough, it is less likely to spin unlike when making rotlis. Continue rolling it out until the folded dough is uniformly about eighth-inch thick. Lightly dust off the uncooked pol'y. The resulting flattened pol'y is generally triangular in shape.

Method: To Cook

Heat a griddle or shallow nonstick pan on medium-high heat. When ready to place the pol'y in the pan, turn it down to medium heat. The side that hits the pan first is the first side. Watch for the dough to bubble slightly and move it around in the pan without flipping it over to avoid hotspots. Turn it over approximately a minute later. The first side should be lightly spotted but not have dark spots. If spots appear too quickly, reduce the heat. Repeat on the second side, and while the second side cooks, lightly baste the first side with ghee. Using a spatula, flip the pol'y and repeat the basting. Both sides should have cooked once without ghee and once with ghee. Remove from heat and cover with a paper towel or a colander to help the steam evaporate. Once they have come to room temperature, the pol'ya can be transferred to an appropriate storage container.

1. Ghee-laminated sheets of dough

2. Partially rolled ghee-laminated dough

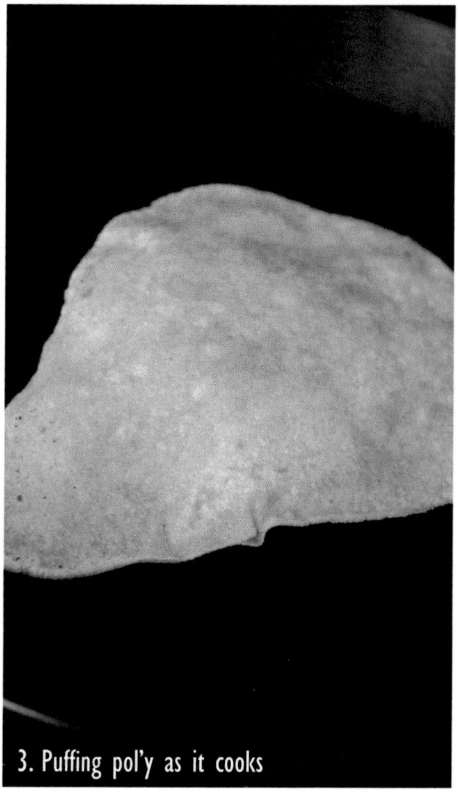

3. Puffing pol'y as it cooks

4. Finished Ghadi-chya-pol'ya

Rice

Rice/Sorghum/Pearl Millet Bhakri

Rustic Griddle-fried Rice/Sorghum/Pearl Millet Bread

Makes: Eight 2-piece servings
Prep Time: Less than 20 minutes
Cook Time: 20 minutes

The coastal regions of India are replete with paddy fields as rice is consumed in various forms across the country. This bhakri is made from rice flour. The dough is a tender, soft and supple one, and the bhakri sops up flavorful and rich coconut-based sauces. It is naturally gluten-free. The same recipe and method can be adapted for sorghum flour or pearl millet flour.

Ingredients

2 cups water
¼ tsp salt
1 tbsp ghee, plus extra for basting
2 cups flour (rice, sorghum or pearl millet), sifted, plus extra for rolling

Method: To Bind

In a large saucepan, boil the water, salt and ghee. As the water boils, turn the heat down and slowly add the flour into the water and stir in as best you can. Once all the flour is in the water, turn off the flame and remove this mixture from the stovetop. Stir this mixture vigorously with a wooden or sturdy spoon until all the water is absorbed. Cover and set aside for 20 minutes until the mixture cools.

Once cooled, uncover the dough and stir to remove any remaining lumps. If there are still some dry spots, stir in two tablespoons of boiled water, and re-cover. If there are no dry spots, turn out the dough onto a lightly flour-dusted clean surface, and using your palm, knead the dough as you would for making bread. This action will massage the dough and make it easier to roll. The dough should be soft but not overly sticky. Divide the dough into 16 pieces, roll them until smooth, and keep covered with a damp cloth.

Method: To Roll

Set aside a small plate of dry rice flour for dredging. Lightly flatten the ball of dough and dredge it through the dry flour. Place this diskette on the rolling surface, and using a tapered rolling pin, roll the dough out slowly and lightly in small circles. Too much pressure will cause the bhakri to stick to your rolling surface. Keep the rolling pin within the edges of the dough; do not "roll out" over the edge, As needed, dredge the flattening diskette carefully in the dry flour. The finished uncooked bhakri should be no more than quarter-inch thick.

Method: To Cook

Heat a shallow non-stick skillet, griddle or crepe pan to medium-high. Sprinkle a few drops of water; if they begin to dance, the pan is ready for use.

Sprinkle water on one side of the uncooked bhakri and place it, wet side down, onto the hot pan. Allow it to cook undisturbed for half-a-minute, then move it around to ensure it does not stick but do not flip it yet. Cook for another half-a-minute or until the lower side develops a few light spots. As the underside begins to cook, there will be a small amount of brown spotting, and small air pockets that form in the bhakri that will give it a pebbled/bubbly look. Check the underside and if a third of the surface is covered in light spots, it is ready to flip over. Sprinkle water on the upper side of the bhakri and flip it over. Let this cook for about 10-15 seconds. Then using a wadded up clean dry kitchen towel, gently press down on the air bubbles on the bhakri to force the trapped air to move around and to ensure the bhakri cooks through. Repeat the cooking process for the second side. The edges will also take on a slight browning and may start curling. This is normal. If either side appears undercooked, return it to the skillet. When both sides are cooked, remove from the pan and baste lightly with ghee or butter. Keep warm until ready to serve. For novices, it will be easier to cook each bhakri as it is rolled out. Turn down the heat between making two bhakris so the skillet does not become too hot.

Sorghum bhakri with milk

Buckwheat & Rice Bhakri

Rustic Griddle-fried Buckwheat and Rice Bread

Makes: Eight 1-piece servings
Prep Time: Less than 20 minutes
Cook Time: 20 minutes

This is a heartier variation on the rice flour bhakri, better suited for novice cooks. The buckwheat flour tends to darken the dough and it may appear less appetizing but it is definitely healthier than the rice flour bhakri. Try your hand at both and see which one you like more!

Ingredients

½ cup water
¼ tsp salt
¼ tbsp ghee plus extra for basting
⅔ cup rice flour, sifted, plus extra for rolling
¼ cup buckwheat flour, sifted

Method: To Bind

Sift both flours together and set aside. Boil the water with pinch of salt &. ghee. When it boils, remove from heat and mix in both flours. Using a large wooden spoon, stir vigorously until all the dry flours are combined in and there are no lumps. Cover and set aside.

When cool enough to handle but still warm, knead the dough gently using the ball of your palm into a smooth ball. Divide the dough into 2" balls, and roll in all the edges to ensure there are no cracks. Cover with a damp cloth until ready to use.

Method: To Roll

Dust each ball with rice flour and roll out gently into quarter-inch-thick bhakris, dusting with dry flour as required (see method in rice bhakri recipe). Work with one uncooked bhakri at a time.

Method: To Cook

Heat a shallow non-stick skillet, griddle or crepe pan to medium-high. Sprinkle a few drops of water; if they begin to dance, the pan is ready for use.

Sprinkle water on one side of the uncooked bhakri and place it, wet side down, onto the hot pan. Allow it to cook undisturbed for half-a-minute. Then move it around to ensure it does not stick but do not flip it yet. Cook for another half-a-minute or until the lower side develops a few light spots. As the underside begins to cook, there will be a small amount of brown spotting, and small air pockets that form in the bhakri will give it a pebbled/bubbly look. Check the underside and if a third of the surface is covered in light spots, it is ready to flip over. Sprinkle water on the upper side of the bhakri and flip it over. Let this cook for about 10-15 seconds. Then using a wadded up clean dry kitchen towel, gently press down on the air bubbles on the bhakri to force the trapped air to move around and to ensure the bhakri cooks through. Repeat the cooking process for the second side. The edges will also take on a slight browning and may start curling. This is normal. If either side appears undercooked, return it to the skillet. When both sides are cooked, remove from the pan and baste lightly with ghee or butter. Keep warm until ready to serve.

Buckwheat & rice bhakri with mushroom & paneer sabzi

Seasoned Griddle-fried Breads

Seasoned griddle-fried breads are often added to light meals when elaborate meals are not expected or when meal time is limited. This section includes both savory and dessert preparations. Most are cooked with a light balance of spices that are flavorful enough for a light meal but delicate enough to not be overwhelming. Typically, the seasonings are kneaded into the dough and it is cooked right away.

A bunch of fresh fenugreek leaves with its signature tripartite leaves are ready for picking.

Methi Thepla

Griddle-fried Fenugreek Paratha

Makes: Eight 2-piece servings
Prep Time: 10 minutes
Cooking Time: 30 minutes

A staple of Western India, thepla is a version of a whole wheat paratha. Traditionally, theplas are intended to be travel-worthy eats and are made with lots of oil, sometimes yogurt, and can often last several days unrefrigerated. This recipe is for the "instant" thepla variety and makes for a quick variation to a meal.

Ingredients

1 tsp cumin seeds
1 tsp ginger paste
1 tsp garlic paste
1 tsp cayenne pepper powder
1 tsp whole black peppercorns, freshly cracked
1 cup fresh fenugreek leaves, see Pre-Prep note
OR 2 tsp kasoori methi or dried fenugreek leaves, crushed
3 cups atta (stone-ground durum whole wheat flour), sifted, plus extra for dredging
¼ cup unflavored Greek yogurt
Salt, to taste
4 tbsp oil for basting

Pre-Prep

If using fresh fenugreek leaves, carefully pick through and use only the leaves from each stem. Rinse and set aside.

Method: To Bind

Use a food processor fitted with an S-blade or a large bowl to combine the cumin seeds, ginger paste, garlic paste, cayenne pepper powder, black pepper and fenugreek leaves. If kneading by hand, finely chop the leaves, else it will be difficult to roll the thepla. If using dried leaves add them to the bowl. Add in flour and salt. Add a few tablespoons of yogurt at a time and pulse or knead until the dough comes together. The dough should be firm but not hard, moist but not wet, and slightly firmer than Play-Doh®. It will be slightly sticky. Remove the dough and cover until ready to roll.

Method: To Roll

Divide the dough into golf-ball-sized pieces. Using the palms of your hands, roll each piece into a smooth ball and lightly flatten to make 1" diskettes. Keep covered to avoid drying.

Roll these out similar to rolling a paratha. As you begin, dredge only the diskette you are going to roll in the dry flour and dust off any excess. Work on a flat, dry rolling surface. Using a tapered rolling pin, gently roll out the dough using light pressure from your fingers (not the palm) to spread the thepla dough. Roll outwards but not over the edge. Dredge/dust with dry flour occasionally, but unlike a paratha, use very little flour - just enough to prevent the dough from sticking to the rolling surface. Lightly dust off the rolled uncooked thepla.

Method: To Cook

Heat a griddle or shallow nonstick pan on medium-high heat. When ready to start cooking the thepla, lower the heat to medium and transfer the rolled uncooked thepla to it. The dough will bubble slightly. Move it around in the pan so that all parts of the thepla cook evenly. Approximately a minute later, turn it over. The first side should be lightly spotted but not have dark spots. If you see dark spots, reduce the heat. Repeat on the second side. At this time, lightly baste the top of the thepla with oil, flip over, baste the second side, and cook both sides until they begin to show tan-brown spots. Both sides should have oil, and be cooked once without oil and once with oil, and there should be no doughy spots. Remove from heat and cover with a paper towel or a colander to let the steam evaporate. Lightly wipe down the pan to remove any burnt flour or excess oil before starting on the next thepla. Once they have come to room temperature, the theplas can be transferred to an appropriate storage container and stored in the refrigerator for up to two days. To reheat, wrap them as a stack in foil and place in a warm oven for 20 minutes, or warm individually on the griddle.

Doodhi Paratha

Seasoned Griddle-fried Bread with Bottle Gourd

Makes: Eight 2-piece servings
Cooking Time: 30 minutes

Bottle gourd or Opo squash is a succulent and tender vegetable that is rich in fiber and vitamins, almost sweet to taste, and takes on flavors easily. Everyone must try this dish at least once.

Ingredients

1 tsp cumin seeds
1 tsp ginger paste
1 tsp garlic paste
1 tsp cayenne pepper powder
1 tsp whole black black peppercorn, freshly cracked
1 cup fresh grated bottle gourd, see Pre-Prep note
3 cups atta (stone-ground durum whole wheat flour), sifted, plus extra for dredging
¼ cup unflavored Greek yogurt or less
Salt, to taste
4 tbsp ghee, melted

Pre-Prep

Choose the smallest tender squash and store it in the fridge until ready to use. Cut the squash into manageable portions, and place the remaining in water. Peel and grate the bottle gourd. Remove any large seeds.

Method: To Bind

In a large bowl combine the cumin seeds, ginger paste, garlic paste, cayenne pepper powder, black pepper and grated bottle gourd along with the juices of the squash. Add the flour, salt and bind firmly. Once all the liquid is absorbed add a few tablespoons of yogurt at a time, kneading a little each time before adding more yogurt. Use only as much as the dough can absorb fully. The finished dough should be firm but not hard, moist but not wet, and slightly firmer than modeling clay. It may be slightly sticky. Cover until ready to roll.

Method: To Roll

Divide the dough into golf-ball-sized pieces. Using the palms of your hands, roll each piece into a smooth ball and lightly flatten to make 1″ diskettes. Keep covered to avoid drying.

Roll these out similar to rolling a fulka rotli, without dredging in the flour after the first dredge. As you begin, dredge only the diskette you are going to roll in the dry flour and dust off any excess. Work on a flat, dry rolling surface. Using a tapered rolling pin, gently roll out the dough using light pressure from your fingers (not the palm) to spread the dough. Roll outwards but not over the edge, until it is about 6″ in diameter. Lightly dust off the rolled uncooked paratha.

Bottle gourd paratha with spicy garlic peanut chutney

Method: To Cook

To cook, heat a griddle or shallow nonstick pan on medium-high heat. Reduce the heat to medium and transfer the rolled uncooked paratha to it. The dough will bubble slightly. Move it around in the pan so that all parts of the paratha cook evenly. Approximately a minute later, turn it over. The first side should be lightly spotted but not have dark spots. If you see dark spots, reduce the heat. Repeat on the second side. At this time, lightly baste the top of the paratha with ghee, flip over, baste the second side, and cook both sides until they begin to show tan-brown spots. Both sides should have ghee, and be cooked once without ghee and once with ghee, and there should be no doughy spots. Remove from heat and cover with a paper towel or a colander to let the steam evaporate. Lightly wipe down the pan to remove any burnt flour or excess ghee before starting on the next one. Once they have come to room temperature, the parathas can be transferred to an appropriate storage container and stored in the refrigerator for up to two days. To reheat, wrap them as a stack in foil and place in a warm oven for 20 minutes, or warm individually on the griddle.

Laal Mooli Paratha

Griddle-fried Red Radish & Scallion Bread

Makes: Eight 2-piece servings
Cooking Time: 30 minutes

An unusual blend, this is an easy one to put together. Fresh red radishes make beautiful specks of color in the finished paratha, their once sharp flavors mellowing down in the cooking process. Finely trimmed scallions add a refreshing bite to the finished dish and it feels like Springtime on a plate when it is served.

Ingredients

1 tsp cumin seeds
1 tsp cayenne pepper powder (optional, or black pepper)
5-8 red radishes, grated
2 stems scallions or green onion, finely sliced
3 cups atta (stone-ground durum whole wheat flour), sifted, plus extra for dredging
¼ cup unflavored Greek yogurt
Salt, to taste
4 tbsp ghee, melted

Method: Dough

In a large bowl combine the cumin seeds, ginger paste, garlic paste, cayenne pepper powder or black pepper and grated radishes and scallions. Add the flour and salt and mix well until any water is absorbed. Add a few tablespoons of yogurt at a time, and knead a little each time before adding more yogurt. The finished dough should be firm but not hard, moist but not wet, and slightly firmer than modeling clay. It may be slightly sticky. Cover until ready to roll.

Method: To Roll

Divide the dough into golf-ball-sized pieces. Using the palms of your hands, roll each piece into a smooth ball and lightly flatten to make 1″ diskettes. Keep covered to avoid drying.

Roll these out similar to rolling a fulka rotli, without dredging in the flour after the first dredge. As you begin, dredge only the diskette you are going to roll in the dry flour and dust off any excess. Work on a flat, dry rolling surface. Using a tapered rolling pin, gently roll out the dough using light pressure from your fingers (not the palm) to spread the dough. Roll outwards but not over the edge, until it is about 6″ in diameter. Lightly dust off the rolled uncooked paratha.

Method: To Cook

To cook, heat a griddle or shallow nonstick pan on medium-high heat. Reduce the heat to medium and transfer the rolled uncooked paratha to it. The dough will bubble slightly. Move it around in the pan so that all parts of the paratha cook evenly. Approximately 1 minute later, turn it over. The first side should be lightly spotted but not have dark spots. If you see dark spots, reduce the heat. Repeat on the second side. At this time, lightly baste the top of the paratha with ghee, flip over, baste the second side, and cook both sides until they begin to show tan-brown spots. Both sides should have ghee, and be cooked once without ghee and once with ghee, and there should be no doughy spots. Remove from heat and cover with a paper towel or a colander to let the steam evaporate. Lightly wipe down the pan to remove any burnt flour or excess ghee before starting on the next one. Once they have come to room temperature, the parathas can be transferred to an appropriate storage container and stored in the refrigerator for up to two days. To reheat, wrap them as a stack in foil and place in a warm oven for 20 minutes, or warm individually on the griddle.

Griddle-fried Stuffed Breads

Stuffed breads or parathas are often consumed as a breakfast or snacks. Many find that they are a great way to make a quick and easy meal. Many prudent chefs use leftover entrees to stuff into the breads for refreshing revisions while others make special fillings for unique takes on an otherwise ordinary preparation. Stuffed breads can be sweet or savory and more often than not, can be made a few days ahead of time.

A partially sealed dumplings for Matarwala Aloo Paratha.

Matarwala Aloo Paratha

Griddle-fried Wheat Bread Stuffed with Potatoes & Peas

Makes: Twelve pieces
Prep Time: 30 minutes
Cook Time: 30-45 minutes

A favorite at breakfast, this is a very filling bread and often served with light sides like a bowl of sweet yogurt, a quick pickle or relish. The filling can be made ahead.

Ingredients: Filling

2 tbsp oil
1-2 tsp cumin seeds
1 tsp fresh ginger paste
1 tsp fresh garlic paste
1 large jalapeño, deseeded and finely chopped (optional)
5-10 fresh curry leaves, chopped coarse (optional)
¼ tsp turmeric powder
1 tsp cayenne pepper powder
2 lbs baking potatoes, boiled, peeled, and mashed
½ cup petite peas, blanched and rinsed
¼ cup fresh cilantro leaves (optional)
Salt, to taste
Sugar, to taste
1 tsp lemon juice

Ingredients: Paratha

One and half measure prepared fulka rotli dough
Wheat flour for dredging
Ghee for basting

Method: Stuffing

Heat 2 tbsp oil in a small saucepan. Add cumin seeds. As they sizzle, add the ginger paste and garlic paste, and sauté for 1-2 minutes. Add the jalapeño and curry leaves, taking care so that they do not jump out of the pan. Add the turmeric powder and cayenne pepper powder, and remove from heat. Allow the spices to cook in their own heat for a few minutes. Transfer this spice oil mixture into a large mixing bowl. Mix in the mashed potatoes, blanched peas and cilantro, if using, and season with salt, sugar and lemon juice. Knead this mixture for a minute until well combined. Check taste for salt. Use a ¾″ or smaller cookie scooper to make portions of the potato mash, and lightly roll each scoop between the palms of your hands to ensure there are no cracked seams. Set these croquette-like balls aside.

Method: To Make Paratha

Divide the dough into 12 equal portions, roll to seal seams, cover and set aside.
Start by rolling out a single ball into a flat disk, as one would begin a paratha, no more than 5″ diameter. Place the mashed potato ball in the center, pinch the dough and fold over the ball to cover the ball completely, like a dumpling. Ensure the seams are sealed. Lightly flatten this in the palm of your hand. Dredge the ball in dry flour and begin to roll again, this time very lightly to ensure the filling does not spill out. Roll to make an 8″ paratha using dry flour to dust as needed. When sufficiently rolled, dust off excess flour and cook on a shallow fry pan, as you would a regular paratha, basting occasionally with ghee. Serve warm.

Paneer Gaajar Paratha

GRIDDLE-FRIED WHOLE WHEAT BREAD WITH CARROTS & PANEER

Makes: Twelve pieces
Prep Time: 30 minutes
Cook Time: 30 minutes

An easy fix with simple ingredients, this paratha offers a mild and sweeter variation to other stuffed breads.

Ingredients: Filling

2 tbsp cooking oil
1 tsp cumin seeds
1 tsp garlic past
2 tsp ginger paste
¼ cup grated carrots
1½ cup paneer, blanched and crumbled
2 tbsp chopped cilantro leaves
1 tsp lemon juice
Salt, to taste

Ingredients: Paratha

1 measure prepared fulka rotli dough
Wheat flour for dredging
Ghee for basting

Method: Filling

Heat oil and temper with cumin seeds. Add ginger paste, and garlic paste and stir well. Allow this to cook for 1 minute and quickly follow with grated carrots. Sauté them for another minute and remove from heat. Mix this into remaining ingredients, season with salt and set aside as stuffing. This can be made a few days ahead of time.

Method: To Make Paratha

Follow the method for making Matarwala Aloo Paratha, replacing the filling with this paneer and carrot filling instead. Cook it as you would the Matarwala Aloo Paratha. Serve warm with a side of your choice.

Phudineywali Paneer Sandwich

Paneer & Mint Toaster Sandwich

Makes: varies
Prep Time: 20 minutes
Cook Time: 10 minutes

Toaster sandwiches may be old fashioned but are very easy to assemble. This is one of my favorite toaster sandwich, stuffed with a creamy and lightly flavored paneer that brings a smile to every face when it comes to the table. Use home-made paneer, or store-bought paneer to make this filling up to three days beforehand. With just a light hint of herbs and spices, it makes for a satisfying snack.

Ingredients: Filling

2 tbsp cooking oil
1 tsp cumin seeds
1 tsp nigella seeds
2 tsp ginger paste
1½ cup paneer, blanched and crumbled
2 tbsp chopped mint leaves
1 tsp lemon juice
Salt, to taste

Ingredients: Sandwich

1 loaf sandwich bread of choice (Italian or other), edges trimmed
2 tbsp melted butter for basting, optional

Method: Filling

Heat oil and temper with cumin and nigella seeds. Add ginger paste and allow this to cook for a minute and quickly follow with grated carrots. Sauté for another minute and remove from heat. Mix this into remaining ingredients, season with salt and set aside as stuffing.

Method: To Make Sandwich

Prepare a sandwich maker (or a panini press) with a light basting of butter. Fill the paneer stuffing within two slices of bread, and place in the sandwich maker. Seal and allow it to cook until the crust is golden, 2-4 minutes depending on the device. Serve hot with Coconut Chutney or even ketchup.

Puran Poli

Griddle-fried Wheat Bread Stuffed with Sweetened Pigeon Peas

Makes: Eight pieces
Prep Time: 20 minutes
Cook Time: 40 minutes

This holiday favorite across most of India but particularly along the west coast is incredibly decadent, rich and luscious. The word Poli means a kind of bread, whereas the word "Puran" refers to any kind of a sweet mushy stuffing. Stuffing ingredients can vary: some communities use skinned and cooked split chickpeas, others prefer pigeon peas. Regardless of how they are made, dousing the warm Puran Polis with a fresh slather of ghee makes for an extra special treat.

Ingredients: Filling

2 tbsp ghee
½ cup split pigeon peas, cooked in 1 cup water until softened
½ cup sugar, or to taste
3-4 green cardamom pods, seeded and finely powdered
2-3 strands of saffron
¼ tsp grated nutmeg

Ingredients: Poli

1 measure prepared fulka rotli dough
Wheat flour for dredging
Ghee, for basting

Method: Filling/Puran

Warm two tablespoons of ghee in a nonstick saucepan. As it melts, add the cooked pigeon peas, and stir until the water evaporates and the mixture thickens. Continually scrape the sides of the saucepan to ensure even distribution of heat or else the daal will burn. Add half the sugar and stir it in well. Adjust to desired sweetness. Reduce the heat and continue to thicken until the mashed pigeon peas resemble mashed potatoes. Add the crushed cardamom powder, saffron and nutmeg, stir well and portion into eight pieces.

Method: To Make Puran Poli

Follow the method for making stuffed Matarwala Aloo Paratha, replacing the savory filling with this sweet pigeon pea filling instead. Cook it in the same manner and finish with a generous basting of melted ghee. Serve warm.

Gul Poli

Griddle-fried Bread Stuffed with Roasted Sesame, Peanuts & Jaggery

Makes: Ten to twelve polis
Prep Time: 20 minutes
Cook Time: 30 minutes

A popular preparation along the west coast of India, this nutty preparation is known to keep well and is often used as a travel snack. The filling can be made up to one week ahead.

Ingredients: Filling

½ lb jaggery, finely grated
¼ cup white sesame seeds, lightly roasted
½ cup raw peanuts, lightly roasted, husked and crushed to a coarse powder
1 tsp white poppy seeds, lightly toasted
¼ tsp nutmeg powder
2-3 green cardamom pods, seeded and finely powdered

Ingredients: Poli

1 measure prepared fulka roti dough
Whole wheat flour for dredging
Ghee for basting

Method: Filling/Puran

In a large bowl mix the jaggery, roasted white sesame seeds, peanut powder, poppy seeds, nutmeg and cardamom powders. Knead lightly to combine. Use a teaspoon to portion out filling for the Gul Poli.

Method: To Make Gul Poli

Follow the method for rolling the roti dough, including the stuffing and cooking as you would for a Matarwala Aloo Paratha. Baste with ghee as the Gul Poli cooks on the griddle, serve warm. Store for up to 1 week in an airtight container.

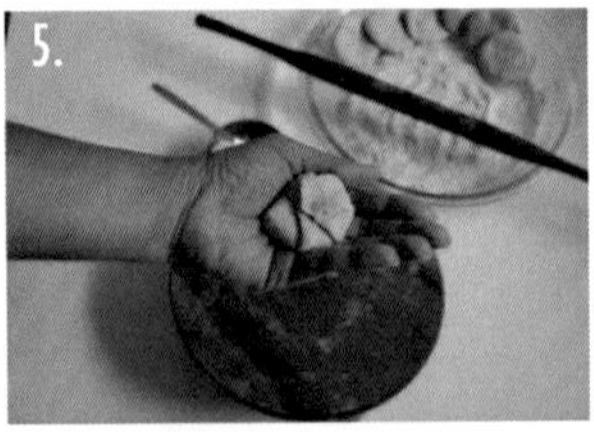

10.
11.
12.
13.
14.
15.

Fried Breads

Fried breads or pooris are perhaps the most popular of the variety of Indian bread in restaurant fare, only next only to naan. These morsels of airy goodness can vary in size – from firm and crunchy puffed pooris for the popular street fare pani poori, to cracker like varieties of masala poori, soft and one-bite dinner pooris and large dinnerplate sized bhaturas. Typically paired with rich sauces, most are easy to make. Here are a few classic varieties.

This variation of the masala poori is made with all purpose flour instead of wheat flour and dotted with fork-marks. It yields a cracker like poori with a longer shelf life.

Poori

Fried Whole Wheat Bread

Makes: Varies
Cooking Time: 30 minutes

The most common of all fried breads is the simple poori. It uses the same dough as a rotli, but simply treating it differently gives a completely different result. Enjoy these as part of a meal, dessert or snack.

Ingredients

1 cup atta (stone-ground durum whole wheat flour), sifted
Water, to bind
1 tsp oil
Salt, to taste
Oil, for deep frying

Method

Combine all the ingredients in a bowl except the oil and knead into a firm dough using enough water. Add half teaspoon of oil and knead again. Set aside for 15 to 20 minutes.

Divide the dough into marble-sized equal portions. Smooth each little portion into a ball and flatten in the palm of your hands, they should be just a bit larger than an inch in diameter. Toss the little diskettes with half a teaspoon of oil to keep them from drying. Cover and set aside. Roll out each portion into a small circle, using a rolling pin or a tortilla press into eighth-inch thick diskettes.

Heat the oil in a fryer, and get it to 350°F or until hot, but not smoking. Maintain the heat until ready to fry. Add between two and three such diskettes to the oil at a time without overcrowding the surface. Let the first (face down) side cook for about half-minute before flipping it over with a spider. The poori will start puffing up. Deep fry each diskette once on each side until they are lightly golden. Remove and drain on paper towel and serve warm.

Poori with Fruit Salaad

Masala Poori

Spicy Crackers

Makes: Six to ten servings
Prep Time: 20 minutes
Cook Time: 5-8 minutes

Another contender for an anytime snack, masala pooris are addictive because of their simplicity. They pair well with chai, a latte-style coffee, crisp white wines and cold beers.

Ingredients

1 cup atta (stone-ground durum whole wheat flour), sifted
¼ tsp turmeric powder
1 tsp cayenne pepper powder
¼ tsp whole black peppercorns, freshly cracked
1 tsp black cumin seeds
Water, to bind
1 tbsp oil
Salt, to taste
Oil, for deep frying

Method

Combine all the ingredients (except the oil for deep frying) in a bowl and knead into a firm dough using just enough water to bind the ingredients. Set aside for 15-20 minutes.

Divide the dough into marble-sized portions. Smooth out the portions by pressing them down in the palms of your hands. Once all portions are smoothed out, toss them gently in a tablespoon of oil, enough to coat completely. Flatten and then roll out each portion into a small disk with a rolling pin or a tortilla press. Heat the oil in a fryer and deep fry each diskette equally on each side until it fluffs up and begins to turn golden brown. Serve warm or store in an airtight container for later.

Bhatura

Fry Bread

Makes: Twelve servings
Prep Time: 20 minutes plus rise time of 1½ hours
Cook Time: 20 minutes

Bhatura is the traditional pairing for sauce-laden dishes like rajma (red beans) and choley (chickpeas). Traditionally made with semolina flour or all-purpose flour, a bhatura is often as large as a dinner plate. The dough is kneaded, allowed to rest and rise, and then large pooris are rolled out. These pooris are then deep fried. Bhaturas are best consumed immediately when they are still hot and crunchy. They will soften and become chewy shortly after they are fried. If you are rushed, use store bought pizza dough instead.

Ingredients

2 cups bread flour or unbleached all-purpose flour, sifted, plus more for rolling
½ tsp sugar
½ tsp instant dry yeast
2 tsp salt
¾ cup warm water
1 tbsp oil, plus 1 tsp extra
Oil, for deep frying
OR
Pre-made pizza dough
Oil, for deep frying

Method: To Bind

Combine the flour, sugar, yeast and salt in the bowl of a stand mixer and combine. While the mixer is running, add the water and 1 tablespoon of oil, and beat until the dough forms into a ball. If the dough is sticky, add additional flour, a tablespoon at a time, until the dough comes together in a solid ball. If the dough is too dry, add some more water, a tablespoon at a time. Scrape the dough onto a lightly floured surface and gently knead into a smooth, firm ball.

If combining by hand, mix the sugar, yeast and half the warm water in a small bowl, and allow the mixture to become frothy. Make a well in the center of the dry flour and slowly pour this frothy yeast mixture in. Make the dough using a little water at a time until the dough comes together, and knead for 2-5 minutes until it becomes a firm ball.

Regardless of how you prepare the dough, grease a large bowl with the extra oil, add the dough, cover the bowl with plastic wrap, and place in a warm place until double in size, about an hour.

If using store-bought or pre-made dough, follow the recipe from here on. Turn the dough out onto a lightly floured surface and divide into twelve equal pieces. Cover the pieces with a clean kitchen towel or plastic wrap and let rest for ten minutes.

Method: To Shape & Cook

Heat oil in a fryer until it reaches 400°F. On a clean surface, flatten each ball of dough into a small diskette, dredge it in the dry flour, and roll out to about a one-eighth inch thick. Dust off any excess flour. Be careful not to have any tears or uneven surfaces on the rolled out dough, as they will cause the bhatura to crack open or crisp unevenly during cooking. Test the oil by dropping a tiny ball of dough into it. If it rises to the top immediately and browns, the oil is too hot. Lower the heat and wait a minute or two. The ball should drop to the bottom first and then rise to the surface gradually. When the oil is hot enough, carefully slide each diskette into the oil. Fry only one bhatura at a time. The diskette will puff up. Flip it over with a spider or slotted spoon to cook the other side. Remove and drain on a paper towel. Bhaturas can be made a few hours in advance if you don't mind them not being crunchy and puffed up. To store, allow the bhaturas to cool completely, and wrap in foil. You can easily warm them back up in an oven set to the lowest temperature for 10-15 minutes and serve immediately.

Jeera Bhopla Poori

Savory Pumpkin Puffs

Makes: Varies
Cooking Time: 30 minutes

A variation of the simple poori with pumpkin added in, they make a wonderfully succulent snack.

Ingredients

1 cup atta (stone-ground durum whole wheat flour), sifted
¼ cup canned pumpkin puree
1 tsp cumin or caraway seeds
¼ tsp cayenne pepper powder
Additional water, to bind
1 tsp oil
Salt, to taste
Oil, for deep-frying

Method

Combine all the ingredients in a bowl except the oil and water. Knead to make sure that all the ingredients are well combined and seasonings are well distributed. Adding a few tablespoons of water at a time, bind this into a firm dough. The dough must be pliable but not mushy, the consistency of a stress ball. Add half a teaspoon of oil and knead again. Set aside for 15 to 20 minutes.

Divide the dough into marble-sized equal portions. Smooth each little portion into a ball and flatten it in the palm of your hands, they should be just a bit larger than an inch in diameter. Toss these pieces in half a teaspoon oil to keep them from drying. Cover and set aside. Roll out each portion into a small circle, using a rolling pin or a tortilla press into eighth-inch thick diskettes

Heat the oil in a fryer to 350°F or until hot, but not smoking. Maintain the heat until ready to fry. Slide two or three diskettes to the oil at a time without overcrowding the surface. Let the first (face down) side cook for about half minute before flipping it over with a spider. The poori will start puffing up. Deep fry each diskette once on each side until they are lightly golden. Remove and drain on paper towel and serve warm.

Cumin, black cumin and caraway seeds are interchangible in this recipe.

God Bhopla Poori

Sweet Pumpkin Poori with Jaggery & Nutmeg

Makes: Varies
Cooking Time: 30 minutes

A regional variation on the pumpkin poori, this one comes from Western India where jaggery is plentiful. Enjoy these as a snack or dessert.

Ingredients

½ tsp grated nutmeg
2 tbsp powdered sugar
1 cup atta (stone-ground durum whole wheat flour), sifted
¼ cup pumpkin puree
3 tbsp grated jaggery (or brown sugar)
Additional water, to bind
1 tbsp ghee
Salt, to taste
Oil for deep-frying

Method

Combine the grated nutmeg and jaggery in a small bowl and set aside. Combine all the remaining ingredients in a bowl except the ghee and water. Knead to make sure that all the ingredients are well combined and seasonings are well distributed. Adding a few tablespoons of water at a time, bind this into a firm dough. The dough must be pliable but not mushy, the consistency of a stress ball. Add half the tablespoon of ghee and knead again. Set aside for 15 to 20 minutes. Divide the dough into marble-sized equal portions. Smooth each little portion into a ball and flatten it in the palm of your hands, they should be just a bit larger than an inch in diameter. Toss these in a half teaspoon of melted ghee to keep them from drying. Cover and set aside. When ready to cook, roll each portion into a small circle, using a rolling pin or a tortilla press into eighth-inch thick diskettes.

Heat the oil in a fryer to 350°F or until hot, but not smoking. Maintain the heat until ready to fry. Slide two or three diskettes to the oil at a time without overcrowding the surface. Let the first (face down) side cook for about half a minute before flipping it over with a spider. The poori will start puffing up. Deep fry each diskette once on each side until they are lightly golden. Remove and drain on paper towel. While they are still warm dust the nutmeg and jaggery mix onto the hot pooris. Serve warm.

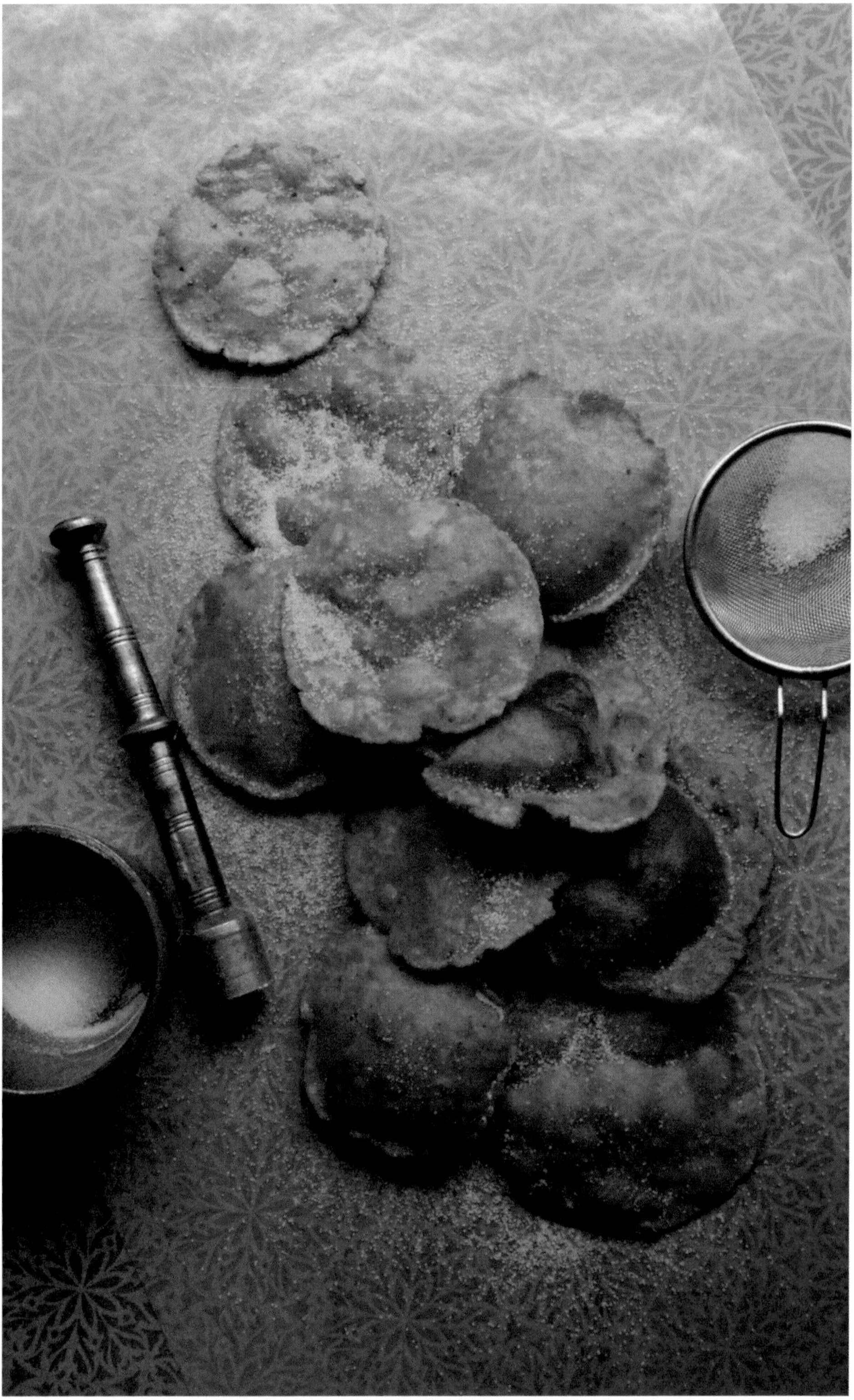

Freehand Breads

These few breads represent different communities of India. Most require a short burst of planning because they need some time to rise or ferment. They are united in their versatile applications and preparation methods – not only can they be made into different shapes and seasoned as per one's liking, they are also welcomed at any time: as a snack, a meal or dessert. Recipes included here extend into more preparations also.

A basket of fresh buttery naans is welcome at any table.

Rice

Idli: Classic Idli, Kanchipuram Idli, Fried Idli & Khaman Idli

Steamed Rice Cake Varieties

Makes: varies
Prep Time: 4-6 hours soak, plus overnight fermentation
Cook Time: <25 minutes

Idlis are made from a fermented batter of rice and lentils that is steamed into pillowy soft cakes. The batter can be set up a day in advance, and a little bit goes a long way. These are just four of dozens of ways to use up the same batter. Enjoy!

Ingredients: Classic Idli Batter

3 cups raw parboiled rice
1 cup raw skinless split urad daal (black gram)
Salt, to taste
1 cup water, to use as needed

Ingredients: Seasoning (optional)

Oil or ghee, as needed
2 tsp black mustard seeds
2 large white onions, finely chopped (optional)
8-10 fresh curry leaves (optional)
¼ cup freshly grated coconut (optional)
Handful of fresh cilantro leaves (optional)
To Serve: Tomato Thekkai or Narial Chutney

Special Tools

Idli pan or shallow silicone cake pan or silicone muffin cups
Stovetop steamer pan set
Aebleskiver (or takoyaki) pan

Pre Prep: Basic Idli Batter

Wash and soak both the rice and the urad daal separately for 4-6 hours. Drain excess water till only enough remains to immerse the grains fully. Use a blender to grind each of them separately into a fine paste in small batches. Add a quarter cup of water at a time, as needed, for smoother grinding. The batter should be thicker than a pancake batter. Both batters will be different in texture; ground rice makes for a grainy batter whereas the lentil batter will be sticky. Combine the two in a deep utensil with at least double the room to allow the batter to rise. The combined batter should be the consistency of a heavy cake batter. Covered with a tight-fitting lid and keep in a warm, dark place overnight to ferment. A draft-free space is ideal. Alternately, a pre-warmed oven that is switched off at 120°F works well too. Place a drip pan underneath to catch any batter that may overflow.

The fermented batter will be light and airy and may double in volume overnight. It may also have a slight sour smell; this is normal. If the batter does not appear to have risen, keep it covered in a warm spot for a few more hours. The batter is typically ready to use within 6-8 hours of the grind, but only if it has fermented and risen. Unused batter, once risen, can be stored in the refrigerator for up to 3 days. Add salt into the batter and mix it very lightly. This batter can be used in one of four preparations below: idli, old fashioned fried idli, Kanchipuram idli, and Khaman idli or Gujarati styled pan-fried idli.

Method: Seasoning

In a small saucepan, heat a tablespoon of oil and add the mustard seeds. Quickly sauté the onions, if using, and curry leaves, and the coconut and cilantro leaves if using. Add it to the batter for Fried Idli or Kanchipuram Idli. Prepare this seasoning without onions if preparing for Khaman Idli.

Khaman Idli (bottom) and Classic Idli with a Chutney Powder dipping sauce

Method: Classic Steamed Idli

Lightly grease the idli pan, the shallow cake pan or the muffin cups. Add water to the bottom of the steamer pan and cover the lid to let steam build up. If using a muffin pan or cake pan, ladle no more than half an inch of batter into the prepared pan, leaving at least a quarter inch room for the batter to rise during steaming. If using an idli pan, ladle just enough to fill the shallow cavity. Gently lower this pan into the steamer basket, cover and cook for 10 minutes or until the steam has evaporated. Remove the pan carefully from the steamer basket. Scoop out the idli from their respective pans using a soft spatula. If using silicone muffin cups, peel the cup away, if using a silicone cake pan, gently run a spatula along the sides to loosen the idli, turn it out onto a dry chopping board, and cut into one-inch squares or diamonds. Regardless of the shape, this idli is ready to eat with a side of your choice.

Method: Old-fashioned Fried Idli

Fill each cavity of an aebleskiver (or takoyaki) pan halfway with oil. Carefully drop dollops of the prepared batter (with or without seasoning) into each cavity, filling halfway. The batter will rise and cook at the same time. Turn each fried idli with a sharp skewer, taking care to not let the oil splash. Fry until each side is golden. Drain on paper towels before serving. Serve hot with sides of choice.

Method: Kanchipuram Idli

Measure out a small quantity of fermented batter into a separate bowl. Each fried idli requires 2-3 tablespoons of fermented batter. Add the seasoning mixture a portion of the batter, and mix in well. It should be light but not runny. Add only a few tablespoons of water to the batter if needed and mix again. Steam as detailed above for a basic batter. Serve hot with sides of choice.

Method: Khaman Idli/Gujarati Styled Pan-Fried Idli

Warm up the seasonings in a large wok or skillet. Add the plain steamed idlis into this seasoning and toss carefully until each piece is coated with spices. Cover and allow this to cook for one minute. Garnish with fresh coconut and cilantro if using. Serve hot with sides of choice.

Rice

Thalipeeth

Griddle-fried Multigrain Cakes

Makes: Twelve servings
Prep Time: 30 minutes
Cook Time: 30 minutes

This dish combines small quantities of three or more kinds of flour into a gluten-free mealtime addition.

Ingredients

1 tsp ajwain seeds (Bishop's weed, optional)
1 tsp sesame seeds
Pinch of asafetida powder
1 tsp cayenne pepper powder
1 cup rice flour, sifted
1 cup besan (chickpea flour), sifted
1 cup skinless split urad daal (black gram) flour, sifted
2 medium onions, finely chopped, see Pre-Prep note
2 cloves garlic, finely minced
¼ cup finely chopped fresh cilantro leaves (optional)
½ cup water, or more as needed
Salt, to taste
1 tsp oil
Ghee or butter, to baste
To Serve: 2 cups unflavored Greek yogurt, whisked smooth

Pre-Prep

Sift all the flours to remove any lumps, mix, and set aside. Place the chopped onions in a sieve or in a cheesecloth and squeeze to remove as much water as possible.

Method: To Bind

In a large bowl or a food processor fitted with an S blade, combine all the dry ingredients. Then add the onions, garlic and cilantro and pulse again. Adding a few tablespoons of water at a time, combine this flour mixture into a tight ball. The flour must be pliable but not soft. Add the oil and pulse or knead one last time. Remove from the food processor, smooth out the creases in the dough and cover it with a damp cloth. Let the dough rest for 15 minutes.

Method: To Shape

Divide the dough into 24 pieces; they may be a little smaller in size than a golf ball. Roll each in the palms of your hands until it is a tight ball, and then flatten out lightly. Lay out a sheet of plastic wrap or aluminum foil on a flat surface. If using aluminum foil, lightly oil it or spray it with nonstick cooking spray. Spread out the dough into a diskette, using light pressure of your fingertips to make each diskette not more eighth-inch thick. Pierce one or two holes in the diskette towards the center for even cooking.

Method: To Cook

To cook, heat a shallow nonstick pan on medium-high heat. When ready to start cooking the thalipeeth, lower the heat to medium and carefully place the uncooked diskette on the pan. Lightly drizzle a few drops of oil along the edges and through the holes so that it cooks evenly. Also move it around on the pan after 1 minute to prevent burn spots. Check the lower side for tan-brown specks; flip once they start to appear. If these appear too quickly, reduce the heat. Repeat on the second side, with a light drizzle of oil. Use the back of a spatula to pat down the thalipeeth during cooking to allow the heat to sear through. Remove from heat and cover with a paper towel or a colander to let the steam evaporate. Lightly wipe down the pan to remove any excess oil before starting on the next thalipeeth. Serve warm with a side of yogurt or yogurt sprinkled with fresh cilantro and a dash of salt.

Thalipeeth with a wilted salad of Enoki mushrooms and radish sprouts in a warm Methkut dressing, paired with plain Greek yogurt on the side.

Ladi Pav

Dinner Rolls

Makes: Twelve servings
Prep Time: 2 hrs 45 minutes
Cook Time: 25 minutes

This is an addictive, simple cross between an Italian roll and a French bread in taste. Pav bread gained popularity in India as a poor man's loaf, but it pairs well with breakfast omelets, or meaty stews.

Ingredients

1½ cups warm water plus ¼ cup
1 tbsp active dry yeast
1 tbsp sugar
4 cups organic bread flour, sifted
1 tsp salt
2 tbsp oil
1 tbsp butter, softened, plus extra for basting

Method: To Bind & Shape

Mix half a cup of warm water, sugar and yeast, and let it to stand for 10 minutes until frothy.
In a large mixing bowl, combine the flour and salt. Make a well in the middle and add in the frothy yeast mixture with one cup of water. Mix well with a wooden spoon until the mixture begins to leave the sides of the bowl. Add the softened butter and oil, and knead, while still in the bowl, into a smooth ball of dough. If the flour appears dry, add a few tablespoons of water at a time to the dough from the extra water and bind it completely into a ball of dough. Prepare a clean surface by dusting it with flour. Transfer the dough onto the surface and knead it for 2 minutes. Make a smooth ball and transfer to a greased bowl. Cover the bowl with a damp napkin and set aside until doubled in size; this may take about one and a half hours.

Method: To Bake

Grease a 9″ x 14″ baking tray. Once the dough has doubled, sprinkle a little flour on a clean surface and divide the dough into twelve equal parts. Shape each part into a ball and place one next to another in the prepared tray. Cover the tray with a wet cloth and allow this to rise again for at least one hour. While the second rise is in progress, preheat the oven to 375°F. Once the rolls have risen, brush them with a little melted butter. Place the finished tray into the preheated oven and bake for 25 minutes or until a light golden glaze appears on the tops. Enjoy hot.

Wada Pav

Hush Puppy Bites

Makes: Twelve servings
Prep Time: 30 minutes
Cook Time: 25 minutes

A popular street fare in India, Wada Pav combines Pav bread (see previous recipe), a spicy hush puppy, called "bonda" or "wada" and a spicy garlic chutney to make an addictive snack or meal.

Ingredients: Bonda/ Wada

2 tbsp oil
1-2 tsp cumin seeds
1″ fresh ginger, finely minced
3-4 garlic cloves, crushed
1 large jalapeño, deseeded and finely chopped (optional)
5-10 fresh curry leaves, chopped coarse
⅓ tsp turmeric powder
1 tsp cayenne pepper powder
2 lbs baking potatoes, boiled, peeled, and mashed
¼ cup fresh cilantro leaves (optional)
Salt, to taste
Sugar, to taste
1 tsp lemon juice

Ingredients: Bonda/ Wada Batter

1 cup besan (chickpea flour), sifted
⅓ tsp turmeric powder
1 tsp cayenne pepper powder
Pinch of baking soda
½ cup water, more as needed
Salt, to taste
4 or more cups oil for frying

Ingredients: To Serve

12 pav breads
1 cup spicy peanut and garlic chutney
¼ cup or more narial chutney (optional)

Pre-Prep: Bonda/Wada

Heat 2 tbsp oil in a small saucepan. Add cumin seeds. As they sizzle, add the minced ginger and garlic, and sauté for 1-2 minutes. Carefully add the jalapeño, if using, and curry leaves. Add the turmeric powder and cayenne pepper powder, and remove from heat. Allow the spices to cook in their own heat for a few minutes. Transfer this spice oil mixture into a large mixing bowl. Mix in the mashed potatoes and cilantro, if using, and season with salt, sugar and lemon juice. Knead this mixture for a minute until well combined. Check taste for salt. Use a 1″ cookie scooper to make portions of the potato mash, and lightly roll each scoop between the palms of your hands to ensure there are no cracked seams. Set these croquette-like balls aside.

Pre-Prep: Batter

Combine the batter ingredients with water and whisk well to remove any lumps. Set aside. This should be thinner than pancake batter but thicker than tempura batter.

Method: Bonda

Heat the oil in a deep fryer until it reaches 400°F. Keep a fryer basket fully immersed in the oil. Use a large serving fork to gently dip each potato ball into the batter, and immediately into the fryer. Do not place them all in the basket first and lower them, as this will create too many drips. Each ball will first sink to the bottom and then rise to the top. Fry until golden, about 2-3 minutes each. Fry 3-5 wadas per batch. Raise the fryer basket to remove the wadas all at once. Drain on a paper towel and keep warm until ready to assemble.

Method: Assembly

Lightly warm the pav. Slice it through the middle into a wedge and spread one teaspoon or more of the peanut garlic chutney on one side and another teaspoon of the narial chutney on the other side, if using. Place a single bonda or wada in this wedge and lightly press down to spread the wada. Serve immediately.

Basic Double Roti/Naan

NAAN

Makes: Twelve servings
Prep Time: 1 hr
Cook Time: 25 minutes

This is an old-fashioned way of referring to a kind of bread that uses leavening. Naan, a now familiar Indian bread is more popular in restaurant fare for its ease in preparation. Enhance this basic recipe with seasonings like garlic, fennel seeds or even nigella seeds – either directly rolled into the dough, or mixed with butter as a basting for added variety.

Ingredients

1 tsp active dry yeast
2 tsp sugar
¾ cup warm water
3 tbsp plain yogurt
2 tbsp extra-virgin olive oil
2 cups all-purpose flour, plus more for rolling
1 tsp salt
⅛ tsp baking powder
Extra water for spraying (in spray bottle)
Melted butter for basting

Method: Dough

Mix yeast, sugar and warm water in a small bowl and let it to stand for 10 minutes until frothy. In a separate container, blend the yogurt and olive oil and set aside. In a large bowl, sift in 2 cups of flour, salt and baking powder. Make a well in the center. Pour in the activated yeast mixture and the yogurt and mix in until the dough begins to come together. Lightly knead it until it is a smooth ball of dough. Cover with plastic wrap or a dry kitchen towel and allow this to double in size, for at least 1 hour.

Method: To Shape & Cook

Place a ceramic pizza stone in the oven and pre-heat the oven to its highest setting before starting.
Pinch out a golf ball sized piece of the risen dough. Dust some flour on a clean dry surface and begin to stretch and the dough. Alternately roll it out with a heavy rolling pin, until it is about 4-5" in diameter. Gently stretch it without tearing until the uncooked naan is a little bigger, perhaps only by a few inches. Place the dough on one palm and sprinkle the exposed dough with water. Carefully place this dough, wet side down onto the ceramic pizza stone. Spray the "up" side with water and switch the oven to low broil mode. The dough will begin to cook within half a minute. Using long tongs or a wooden spatula, flip the naan as soon as the upper surface begins to have a few tan spots. Do not spray any water on this naan. Allow this to cook for another half a minute or until a few tan spots begin to appear. Remove carefully from the oven and quickly baste it with melted butter.

Double Roti Pizza

Naan Pizza

Makes: Twelve servings
Prep Time: 30 minutes (more if starting from scratch)
Cook Time: 25 minutes

This is a great way to make a simple meal out of an even simpler dough, naan. Make the dough and toppings ahead of time or use store-bought pizza dough for an even easier preparation. Make individual naan pizzas to allow customizing.

Ingredients: Toppings

1 tbsp oil
½ cup finely chopped red onion
¼ tsp minced ginger
¼ tsp minced garlic
½ tsp garam masala
1 tsp cayenne pepper, or to taste
½ cup finely diced raw chicken meat
or 1 cup sliced crimini mushrooms
1 tbsp tomato paste
or 1 Roma tomato, finely chopped
Salt, to taste
2 tbsp finely chopped cilantro leaves (optional)

Ingredients: Assembly

1 portion naan dough (see previous recipe)
2 tbsp white flour or cornmeal for dusting
½ cup or more grated mozzarella cheese
¼ cup crumbled paneer (optional)
1 tbsp melted butter

Method: Toppings

Heat the oil in a small saucepan. Sauté the onions, ginger and garlic until they have softened. Add the garam masala and cayenne pepper, stir in and add the raw chicken meat or mushrooms. Allow this to cook for 5-10 minutes on low heat until the chicken is cooked. Add the tomato paste or tomatoes, salt and cilantro leaves, stir in and let this cook until all the water has evaporated. Set aside until ready to use.

Method: Assembly

Preheat the oven to 400°F. Lightly dust a large ceramic pizza stone with the flour or cornmeal and begin to stretch or roll the naan dough onto the surface until it reaches the desired size. Baste the edge of the "pizza" with the melted butter. Spread a light layer of mozzarella cheese onto the surface of the "pizza," layer with the toppings. Add the crumbled paneer cheese if using, and the remaining mozzarella cheese. Bake in the preheated oven for 8-10 minutes until the cheese is bubbly. If the edge looks underdone, broil for 1 minute on a low broil. Remove, cut into wedges. Serve immediately.

Anda Bread

Challah

Makes: One large loaf
Prep Time: 10 minutes plus 3 hours to rise
Cook Time: 45 minutes

It would be impossible to ignore the Jewish communities in India and the contributions they make to the food scene. Although Rice Bhakri is often prepared for Sabbath, many who have access to ovens or bakeries include Challah bread in their Sabbath observances. Made with egg, the traditional Jewish Challah bread however is available only in small Jewish bakeries and seldom seen alongside other breads in regular bakeries. Slightly sweeter than ordinary white loaves, this classic recipe is open to adaptation. Make it into rolls or a braided loaf.

Ingredients

¾ tsp yeast
2 tsp sugar
¼ cup luke warm water
2¾ cup all-purpose flour
½ tsp salt
⅓ cup lukewarm water
2 tbsp butter, softened
1 beaten egg yolk

Method

Dissolve yeast in the quarter cup of lukewarm water with sugar. Allow this to rise in a warm place.

Sift flour and salt together and slowly knead in the soft butter. Add yeast solution to dough and make a soft dough with the remaining lukewarm water. Cover with a damp cloth and leave in a warm place for at least 2 - 2½ hours to double in size. Knead again and divide the dough into 3 equal parts. Cover with a damp cloth and leave in a warm place for another hour.

Preheat oven to 350°F. On a floured surface roll each of the dough portions into a long sausage-shaped log. Pinch one end of them together at one end and braid the remaining strands. Tuck in the ends to make sure the ends do not unfurl while baking. Place the braided bread on a greased cookie sheet and brush the surface with the beaten egg yolk. Bake about 40 - 45 minutes, or until golden color. Cool on a wire rack.

Bread Pudding

Challah Bread Pudding

Makes: Twelve servings
Prep Time: 10 minutes
Cook Time: 20-30 minutes

Any day-old sweet bread works for this pudding but Challah bread makes for a particularly delicious one.

Ingredients

1 tbsp butter, melted
2 cups whole milk
¼ cup packed brown sugar, or to taste
¼ cup cream (optional)
1 tsp vanilla
3 large eggs, whisked
¼ cup golden raisins (optional)
¼ cup chopped pecans or walnuts (optional)
1 loaf of Challah bread cut into ½" squares

Method

Preheat oven to 350°F. Grease a 9" X 16" rectangular baking dish with butter, set aside. Warm the milk in a large saucepan, add the sugar in and let the sugar dissolve. Bring this to room temperature before proceeding. Once the milk is cool, add the cream if using, vanilla, and whisked eggs, stir well and set aside. Place the trimmed bread in the prepared baking dish. Sprinkle on golden raisins if using any. Pour the egg and cream mixture over it until all the pieces are coated and soaking. Sprinkle with chopped nuts if using any. Bake for 20-30 minutes until the egg mixture has set. Set it to cool on a wire rack. Serve warm or cold.

Batter

I
f you are familiar with making pancakes, this section will be a breeze. Most batters come from combining a few ingredients with water or a liquid, and then working the dollops on to a griddle.

Aapam/hoppers served with a bowl of sweetenned coconut milk makes a popular breakfast.

Dosa

Home-style Lentil and Rice Crepes

Makes: Eight or more servings
Prep Time: Nil if using Idli batter recipe
Cook Time: <25 minutes

Dosas are a staple for breakfast, and even dinner in Southern India. Dosas require some pre-planning but they are welcomed as they are easy to make once the batter is in place. Restaurant-style dosas, or the thin and crispy variety, are faster to make than thick dosas. The best dosas are the thickness of thin pancakes or fat crepes.

Ingredients

One measure Idli batter from earlier recipe
Oil or ghee, as needed

Method: Batter if making from scratch

Prepare the batter using the idli recipe.

Method: To Make Dosa

To make dosas, ladle out a small quantity of fermented batter into a separate bowl. Each dosa requires quarter cup of fermented batter. Add a little water to bring this fermented batter to pancake batter consistency, and salt to taste, mix very lightly.
Heat a nonstick skillet. Wipe down the hot skillet with a little oil. Drop a ladle full of the thinned-out batter on the skillet and spread quickly in a circular motion with the back of the ladle to be as thin or thick as desired. Drizzle a little oil or ghee all around the edges and let the dosa cook uncovered on medium heat. If preparing a thick dosa, cover the skillet to allow the dosa to steam cook. When the edges begin to separate from the skillet, the dosa is ready to be turned over. Cook in the same manner on the other side, but for half the time as the first. Gently slide the dosa off the skillet onto a serving plate. Serve hot with suitable accompaniment like a stew, a coconut chutney or a daal.

Steps: Homestyle Dosa & Homestyle Dosa with Egg

1. Pour batter

2. Spread batter

3. Drizzle oil/ghee

4. Flip

5. Homestyle dosa

4. Pour cracked egg

5. Season, cover & cook in steam

6. Homestyle dosa with egg

Onion Uttappam

Homestyle Rice and Lentil Crepes with Chopped Onions

Makes: Varies
Prep Time: Nil if using Idli batter
Cook Time: 20 minutes

Day-old dosa batter is used to make uttappam. It also originates in Southern India and although made with dosa batter, it is different because the batter is sourer, and the crepe is topped with vegetables that caramelize during the cooking process. This hearty, gluten-free crepe can be personalized, in this case with chopped onions.

Ingredients: Batter

One measure Idli batter from earlier recipe

Ingredients: Toppings

½ red bell pepper, slivered
1 large onion, cut into rings
Whole black peppercorns, cracked, to taste
Handful of cilantro leaves
2 large tomatoes, cut into rings
Oil for drizzling
To Serve: Green Mango & Coconut Chutney

Method

Heat a shallow griddle or skillet until hot and wipe with a little oil. Spread one ladleful of batter on the hot surface in a circular motion. This batter should spread about quarter-inch thick. Drizzle a teaspoon of oil along the edges and let it cook on medium-low heat. Just before the upper surface sets in, add your selection of toppings, such as tomatoes, bell peppers, onion rings, cilantro etc., in a single layer on top. Cover and allow this to cook in the steam for about a minute. Uncover and flip the uttappam carefully, drizzle the sides with oil, and cook for about half minute. Serve with Green Mango & Coconut Chutney, Chutney Powder, or other accompaniment of your choice.

Dosa with Quick Kumquat Relish

Onion Uttappam with Black Urad Chutney Powder

Maida Sooji Dosa or Campus Dosa

Quick Flour & Semolina Crepes

Makes: Four 2-piece servings
Prep Time: 10 minutes + 20-30 minutes soak
Cook Time: 15 minutes

This dosa, traditionally called maida sooji dosa is an easy fix on busy days as it is made from an unfermented batter and is fairly foolproof.

Ingredients:Batter

1 cup unbleached all-purpose flour, sifted
1 cup fine semolina
½ tsp salt, or to taste
Water, for batter, as required

Ingredients: Tadka/ Seasoning

1 tsp oil
1 tsp cumin seeds
½ tsp whole black peppercorns
10 fresh curry leaves
1 jalapeño, finely chopped
Oil for cooking

Pre-Prep

In a large mixing bowl, combine the all-purpose flour, semolina and salt with water to make a smooth batter. Add in the spice tempering (if adding) and stir until well combined. Set aside for 20-30 minutes.
In a small skillet, heat 1 tsp of oil, add cumin seeds, and allow these to release their flavors. Turn this down to a low heat. Add the curry leaves and jalapeño and stir briefly, allowing the flavors to get absorbed in the oil. Remove from heat and add to the batter. This is the spice tempering. Skip this step if you are short on time.

Method

Heat a shallow griddle or skillet until hot and wipe with a little oil. For each dosa, take a small ladleful of the batter and spread evenly and lightly. The batter should spread less than quarter-inch thick. Drizzle a little oil along the edges. Turn down the heat, and cook for about 2 minutes; flip to cook the other side. Serve hot with garlic chutney or accompaniment of your choice. Store-bought chutney powder served with a few drops of cooking oil is also a common and makes for an easy last-minute pairing. These dosas do not store well.

Campus Dosa drizzled with a pod/chutney powder dressing

Mung Paserattu

Split Yellow Mung Bean Crepe

Makes: Four 2-piece servings
Prep Time: 6 hours pre-soak + 10 minutes prep
Cook Time: 30 minutes

A variation of the rice and lentil dosa, this one is denser in texture by comparison. It does not rise as much as the dosa batter but it tastes just as delicious.

Ingredients: Batter

2 cups raw rice, see Pre-Prep note
1 cup raw skinless split yellow mung bean daal, see Pre-Prep note
2 tsp cumin seeds
1 large onion, finely chopped
1″ fresh ginger, julienned
¼ tsp finely chopped jalapenos (optional)
¼ tsp turmeric
1 tsp salt
¼ cup cilantro, chopped (optional)
Oil for cooking

Pre-Prep

Wash and soak the rice and the daal separately for 6 hours. Rinse, drain and grind them separately to a smooth paste, then combine. The batter should be slightly thinner than muffin batter. Add in all the ingredients and mix well until ready to use.

Method

Heat a shallow griddle or skillet until hot and wipe with a little oil. Use a large ladle to spread the batter into a circular shape on the skillet. The batter will be thick. Cook over low heat for 3-4 minutes until the edges begin to release. Turn the dosa over and drizzle oil along the edges again, and let it cook until crisp all around and golden brown in color. Serve hot with yogurt, coconut chutney or other sides of choice.

Mung Paserattu topped with mustard sprouts and black grapes, with a podi/chutney powder dressing

Adai

Griddle-fried Rice & Chickpea Cakes

Makes: Four 2-piece servings
Prep Time: 4 hours pre-soak + 10 minutes prep
Cook Time: 20 minutes

This is a preparation of soaked and ground skinless chickpeas, or Bengal gram, and rice and combines the flavors of fresh ginger, fresh coconut, dried red chilies and sautéed onions. This gluten-free pancake is best complimented with a bowl of yogurt sweetened with honey and ginger, but you may choose to serve it with unflavored yogurt instead.

Ingredients: Batter

2 cups raw Basmati or Sona Masoori rice, see Pre-Prep note
1 cup raw chana daal (skinless split Bengal gram/chickpeas), see Pre-Prep note

Ingredients: Tadka/ Seasoning

4 tbsp oil
2 tsp cumin seeds
1 large onion, finely chopped
1″ fresh ginger, julienned
10-12 fresh curry leaves
4 whole dried red chilies, broken
¼ tsp asafetida powder
2 tsp whole black peppercorns
¼ cup fresh coconut (scraped)
1 tsp salt
¼ cup cilantro, chopped
Oil for cooking

Pre-Prep

Wash and soak the rice and the daal separately for 4-5 hours. Drain and grind the rice and daal separately to a smooth paste, then combine. The batter should be slightly thinner than muffin batter.

In a small, shallow skillet, heat 2 tablespoons of oil. Add the cumin seeds and let them sizzle briefly. Then add the onions, ginger, curry leaves, red chilies, asafetida powder and whole black peppercorns. When the onions have softened, reduce the heat and add the fresh coconut and salt. Stir for a minute or so until the coconut takes on a lightly golden color. Remove from heat, stir in the chopped cilantro, and set aside to cool. Combine the spice compote with the batter and correct for salt.

Method

Heat a shallow griddle or skillet until hot and wipe with a little oil. Use a large ladle to spread the batter into a circular shape on the skillet. The batter will be thick. Make a hole in the center and pour in quarter teaspoon of oil and drizzle a few drops along the edges. Cover and cook over low heat for 3-4 minutes until the edges begin to release. Turn the adai over and drizzle oil along the edges again, and let it cook until crisp all around and golden brown in color. Serve hot with the plain yogurt, shrikhand, or honey ginger yogurt.

Besan Poora with Onions

Chickpea Crepe with Onions

Makes: Four 2-piece servings
Prep Time: 10 minutes
Cook Time: 15 minutes

Besan is the Hindi name for chickpea flour, and poora is a colloquial term for pancake. The earthy taste of the chickpea flour is delightfully balanced with fresh ingredients like onions, cilantro and tomatoes. Adding eggs increases its protein content but can be skipped to accommodate dietary restrictions.

Ingredients

½ tsp cumin seeds
1 medium white onion, finely chopped
½ tsp cayenne pepper powder
1½ cup besan (chickpea flour), sifted
1½ tsp salt
1 cup water
½ cup fresh cilantro leaves, washed and finely chopped
1 egg, beaten (optional)
½ onion, sliced into rings
Oil for drizzling

Method

In a large mixing bowl, combine the cumin seeds and cayenne pepper powder. Add the besan and salt, and mix thoroughly. Slowly add water, third of a cup at a time, and using a whisk, stir well until there are no lumps in the batter. The batter should be thinner than pancake batter but heavier than crepe batter. Just before you are ready to make the first poora, add the chopped onions, cilantro leaves and beaten egg (if using), and combine again. This batter tends to settle, so stir it regularly to maintain consistency.

Heat a shallow griddle or skillet until hot and wipe with a little oil. Pour one large ladleful of batter onto the hot surface. The batter should spread about eighth-inch thick. Place a few onion rings on to the poora. Drizzle the sides of the poora with oil, as needed, and cook on both sides until golden. Serve hot.

Zucchini & Carrot Besan Poora with Dill

Zucchini & Carrot Crepe with Dill

Makes: Four 2-piece servings
Prep Time: 10 minutes
Cook Time: 15 minutes

A variation on the traditional Besan Poora, this crepe combines sweet and delicate zucchini with a sprinkling of dill that gives it a unique bite and flavor.

Ingredients

½ tsp cumin seeds
1 medium white onion, finely chopped
¼ tsp cayenne pepper powder
½ cup peeled and grated zucchini
½ cup peeled and grated carrots
¼ cup fresh dill leaves, washed and coarsely chopped
1½ tsp salt
1 cup water
1 egg, beaten (optional)
1½ cups besan (chickpea flour), sifted
Oil for cooking

Method

In a large mixing bowl, combine the cumin seeds, white onion, cayenne pepper powder, zucchini, carrots and dill and mix well. Then add the beaten egg, if using, and mix again. Slowly fold in besan and salt. Slowly add water, third of a cup at a time, and using a whisk, stir well until there are no lumps in the batter. The batter should be thinner than pancake batter but heavier than crepe batter. This batter tends to settle, so stir it regularly to maintain consistency.

Heat a shallow griddle or skillet until hot and wipe with a little oil. Pour one large ladleful of batter onto the hot surface. The batter should spread about eighth-inch thick. Drizzle the sides of the poora with oil, as needed, and cook on both sides until golden. Serve hot.

Ghawan

Plain Whole Wheat Crepes

Makes: Four 2-piece servings
Prep Time: 10 minutes + 10 minutes soak
Cook Time: 20 minutes

Although I attribute it to Western India, there are different variations of this across the country with different names. Serve hot off the skillet and they will keep coming back for more. Ghee adds a depth of flavor but can be replaced with a suitable alternate if limited by dietary restrictions.

Ingredients

1 cup atta (stone-ground durum whole wheat flour), sifted
Water, for batter, as required
Salt, to taste
Oil for drizzling, or ghee as needed

Method

In a large mixing bowl, make a thin batter using the whole wheat flour, water and salt. Whisk well to avoid lumps. The batter should be as thick as a creamy soup. Set aside for 10 minutes. Do not let sit more than 10 minutes, because the batter will start to darken and become increasingly sticky.

Heat a shallow griddle or skillet until hot and wipe with a little oil. Drop a ladleful of batter on the griddle and very lightly, spread it in a circular motion. The batter should spread about one eighth inch thick. Drizzle a little ghee all around the edges, cover, and let the crepe cook on medium low heat on each side until golden. The oil or ghee keeps the ghaawan from sticking, whereas the ghee also improves the flavor. Serve hot with a stew of choice.

Malpua

Rose-flavored Wheat Crepes

Makes: Four 2-piece servings
Prep Time: 10 minutes
Cook Time: 20 minutes

Traditional malpuas from the western Indian region of Rajasthan are luscious morsels of wheat flour, deep fried in ghee and doused with sugar syrup. This is a simpler home-style version of malpua with both crunchy corners and a soft center.

Ingredients

⅔ cup whole milk
4 tbsp sugar
½ tsp green cardamom powder
1 cup atta (stone-ground durum whole wheat flour), sifted
1 tsp rose water
4-5 tbsp ghee, for cooking

Pre-Prep

Warm the milk, and dissolve the sugar and cardamom powder into it. Reheat the milk if necessary to ensure all the flavors are extracted well into the milk. Allow it to cool. Place the wheat flour in a large mixing bowl and run a dry whisk through it to ensure there are no lumps. Make a well in the center. Slowly add the milk mixture and whisk until smooth and well combined. This may take 1-2 minutes of constant whisking by hand. Once smooth and creamy, add the rose water. Set aside for 10 minutes to allow the gluten to activate well.

Method

Prepare a skillet with half a tablespoon of ghee and heat. Ensure it spreads all over the pan. Pour the batter carefully in the center of the pan in a single, slow, steady stream. This will allow the batter to distribute organically on the pan and create a wonderful latticed texture on the underside of the crepe. Resist the temptation to smooth the batter over. Cover and turn the heat to low. The steam will par-cook the upper side. After a minute or so, check the edges of the crepe; they should release from the sides. If not, add a little ghee along the edges and let the edges crisp up. Carefully lift the crepe and turn it over. Cook until both sides are golden. Serve immediately with fresh whipped cream and fruits.

Aapam/Hopper

Rice & Tapioca Crepe with Sweetened Grated Coconut & Caramel Sauce

Makes: Four 2-piece servings
Prep Time: 4 hours soak + 10 minutes prep
Cook Time: 20 minutes

A decadent and unexpected treat, this is a variation of a crepe found in Malaysia, Southern India and Sri Lanka. The prep time is worth the wait.

Ingredients: Sweetened Grated Coconut

1 tbsp ghee
1 cup grated coconut, fresh
3-5 tbsp brown sugar or jaggery to taste

Ingredients: Pancake

2 eggs, beaten
2 cups rice flour
¼ cup micro-tapioca pearls, see Pre-Prep note
¼ cup or more coconut milk
¼ tsp of salt
¼ tsp baking powder
¼ tsp finely ground star anise
Water for boiling, extra as needed
Ghee for cooking
1 cup sweetened grated coconut to serve
3-4 tbsp caramel sauce (optional)

Pre-Prep & Method: Sweetened Grated Coconut

Fresh grated coconut is the best for this, however the next best alternate is frozen coconut. Thaw the coconut. In a small saucepan, warm a tablespoon of ghee and roast the coconut until it is lightly golden in color. Add the sugar or jaggery to taste. This can be made ahead of time and stored in the refrigerator. Use within the week.

Pre-Prep: Pancake

Soak the tapioca pearls for 3-4 hours in about 2 cups of water. Drain the water away and cook them in 2 more cups of water until they are soft and don't have a hard core, about 2-3 minutes.

Method

In a large bowl, combine the eggs, rice flour, coconut milk, salt, baking powder and star anise powder, and mix well. Drain the cooked and cooled tapioca pearls and add them in. Whisk thoroughly until the mixture is homogeneous. Set aside for a few minutes until the tapioca absorbs any more liquid, mix again. Thin out with more coconut milk or water.

Heat a shallow non-stick griddle or skillet and wipe down with a little ghee. Pour about quarter cup of the batter into the griddle and tip it around a little to spread the batter evenly. Turn the heat down to medium low and cover with a clear lid. The pancake will cook in its own steam. When the top of the pancake appears set, turn it over and repeat the cooking process. Drizzle a little ghee if the pancake appears dry. Serve warm topped with the sweetened grated coconut drizzled with caramel sauce.

Kheer Patishapta

Bengali Crepes with Kheer

Makes: Four 2-piece servings
Prep Time: 30-40 minutes prep
Cook Time: 15-20 minutes

This is a variation on a delicious and easy dessert recipe, Patishapta, popular in the eastern Indian state of West Bengal. These crepes are inspired by those, except served with a dense, creamy sauce, also known as kheer, made the old-fashioned way, by lovingly reducing the milk on a low flame. Although this recipe calls for one crepe per person, you may enjoy more than a single piece.

Ingredients: Sauce

4 cups whole milk
¼ cup sugar, to taste
¼ cup mixed chopped nuts (optional)

Ingredients: Crepe

2 cups all-purpose flour
2 tbsp semolina
4 tbsp rice flour
½ cup milk
2-4 tbsp ghee for cooking
4-5 tbsp chopped nuts to garnish, optional
¼ cup dried roses to garnish (optional)

Pre-Prep: Kheer/Sauce

In a large heavy bottom saucepan, bring the milk to a boil on low heat. Stir constantly until the milk thickens. Keep stirring until the liquids have thickened past the heavy cream consistency, to about half a cup of liquid. Take great care to not burn the milk. If that happens, start afresh. Once the milk has thickened and reduced by half, add in the sugar to taste and sprinkle the nuts. This kheer can be made ahead.

Method

In a large bowl, combine the all-purpose flour, semolina and rice flour with milk. Stir and set aside.

Heat a shallow non-stick griddle or skillet until hot and wipe with a little gheee. Pour about quarter cup of the batter into the griddle and tip it around a little to spread the batter evenly. Turn the heat down to medium low and cover the crepe with a clear lid. The crepe will cook in its own steam. When the top of the crepe appears set, turn it over and repeat the cooking process. Drizzle a little ghee if the crepe appears dry. Cook evenly on each side for 2 minutes or less.

To Serve

Warm the kheer. Gently fold each crepe, one per person, into a quarter. and spoon a generous portion of kheer over it. Garnish with chopped nuts and dried roses if desired.

Sides: Chutneys, Raitas & More

Most kinds of breads need a pairing that helps make a meal. It can be as simple as a hot cup of cha to dip into, a small chutney on the side or something to dress it up a bit. Although most sides are savory, some can be sweet. This is a mere sampling of the many dishes worthy of accompanying any of the many delicately prepared breads.

Seasonal fruits often become part of a meal in pickles, chutneys or as in this case, Gol Keri.

Masala Cha

Indian Masala Tea

Makes: Two servings
Prep Time: 2 minutes
Cook Time: 5-8 minutes

A cup of steaming hot cha is often a staple pairing for most of the breads mentioned in this book. The fresh ginger and mint offer a refreshing aroma to the cha, enticing everyone even before the cha comes to the table.

Ingredients

1¾ cup water
1 sliver of fresh ginger root (optional)
4 tsp sugar, or to taste
1 tbsp Orange Pekoe tea leaves
1 tsp Earl Grey or other fragrant black tea leaves
¼ cup cold whole milk
2 mint leaves (optional)

Method

Place the water in a large saucepan, add the fresh ginger root, sugar and tea leaves. Bring this to a boil, until the water turns a golden tan color. Add cold whole milk and mint leaves into this. When it comes to a boil, remove from the stove and strain into cups. Serve steaming hot with any savory bread.

Kairywali Naralchi Chutney

Green Mango & Coconut Chutney

Makes: Eight servings
Prep Time: <30 minutes
Cook Time: <20 minutes

Tart, fresh and luscious, any dish paired with this simple chutney is transformed into a tropical delicacy. Fresh ingredients are absolutely essential to this chutney, and though frozen versions are a common substitute, they do not make the chutney as tender or desirable as the one made with fresh ingredients. Keep a watch for firm, green mangoes at the ethnic foods store. Eliminate the mango to create the essential classic coconut chutney.

Ingredients

1 tsp cumin seeds
1″ fresh ginger
1 jalapeño (optional), seeded
½ small raw mango, diced into small pieces, see Prep-Prep note
1 husked coconut, see Prep-Prep note
1 cup fresh cilantro leaves, washed
¼ tsp sugar
Splash of lemon juice
Salt, to taste

Pre-Prep: To Extract Mango Flesh

Wash the raw mango and dry it well with a paper towel. Using a sharp knife, cut away at the outer flesh, keeping the skin, as you would a pitted fruit until you reach the large inner seed. Check for tartness. If the mango is too tart, use only half the mango. Roughly dice the raw mango pieces for the next step.

Pre-Prep: To Extract Fresh Coconut Flesh

Rinse out the coconut to remove any loose husk fibers. Pat dry with a paper towel. Using a hammer, tap along the scored portion of a husked coconut over a bowl until it shows signs of cracking. It may take a few tries to crack the fresh coconut. Once cracked, break the outer shell away, over a bowl, using the hammer. The coconut water will spill out as it cracks in half it is slightly cloudy and must have a sweet fragrance and taste. There are two parts to each coconut half. The coconut flesh is the soft white part. Separating this from the shell is a thin darker outer skin that is not visible when you crack the coconut open. If there is a putrid smell to the coconut flesh or coconut water, all of it must be discarded. Start with a fresh new coconut.

Use a sharp paring knife to carefully trim the white flesh out. This will show off the two parts of the coconut flesh: the white flesh and its dark brown skin. Use a sharp vegetable peeler to scrape and remove the outer dark brown skin. Chop the white flesh into small bite-sized pieces. Rinse and set aside. The water from a good coconut is a refreshing tasty drink.

Method

In a medium food processor bowl, combine the cumin seeds, ginger, jalapeño, 1 cup of coconut flesh bits, the flesh bits from the mango, cilantro, lemon juice, sugar, salt and quarter cup water. Blend on medium-low until it is an even mixture. Thin out with water as needed. Check for salt and spice, and adjust as needed. Store this chutney in a clean, dry glass jar. This chutney can be stored for up to 3 days in the refrigerator or 4 weeks in the freezer.

A traditional coconut grating tool, a vili is a sickle shaped device with a fan-like grater tip.

Cranberry Chutney

Hot Cranberry-Cherry Sauce

Makes: Twelve servings
Prep Time: 10 minutes
Cook Time: 30 minutes plus cooling time

Indian cuisine boasts of many sauces, chutneys, preserves and compotes, but none like this one, a variation of a traditional fresh plum chutney. This one combines warm flavors and becomes unmatched in any store-bought version. A little time spent to cook up this delicious sauce results in many delicious meals.

Ingredients

1 lb fresh organic cranberries
Water, to cover cranberries
½ cup dried cherries, chopped
2″ fresh ginger, finely minced
4 cloves
½ cup packed light brown sugar
½ tsp cinnamon powder

Method

In a medium stockpot, add just enough water to cover the cranberries and cherries and bring to a boil. Continue to cook on high heat until the liquid has reduced to half, about 10 minutes. The cranberries will pop open and the cherry bits will soften. Stir in the minced ginger and cloves. Reduce the heat and continue to cook for another 10 minutes. The mixture will reduce even further. Next, add the brown sugar a few tablespoons at a time and stir in until fully dissolved. Continue to cook for another 10 minutes until the mixture reduces to a sauce-like consistency. In the last few minutes, add the cinnamon powder and continue to cook, covered this time to retain the aroma. Stir occasionally to prevent from sticking. Remove from heat, uncover, and let the steam evaporate. While still warm, transfer the sauce into a sterilized and cooled jar, and allow this to cool on a wire rack. Cap and seal the jar when completely cooled and store in the refrigerator. This sauce can be made ahead of time and remains good to eat for about a week if refrigerated.

Kakdi Koshimbir

Persian Cucumber & Roasted Peanut Chutney

Makes: Twelve servings
Prep Time: 20 minutes
Cook Time: 10 minutes

This is one of my favorite chutneys from western India, this simple side give a new twist to roasted peanuts.

Ingredients

1 tsp ghee
1 tsp cumin seeds
½ tsp freshly grated ginger
1 cup unsalted skin on peanuts, see Pre-Prep note
¼ cup Greek yogurt
2 Persian cucumbers, peeled and finely diced
1 tsp sugar
Salt, to taste
10-12 cilantro stems with leaves, finely minced

Pre-Prep

Dry roast the peanuts until the skin has blistered and parts of the skin start to fall away. Allow them to cool. Slowly rub the peanuts between your palms to loosen the skin. Carefully winnow the skins away until only the peanuts remain. Coarsely grind and set aside.

Method

Warm up ghee in a medium saucepan. Add the cumin seeds and allow them to perfume the ghee. Add the ginger and sauté until the flavors are released. Remove from heat.

While the ghee is still warm, add the crushed peanuts and stir to coat them in the spices. Add the yogurt, Persian cucumbers, sugar and salt and mix in well until all the cucumbers are covered. Garnish with cilantro and serve immediately.

Dahi Chataka

Jalapeños-Mint Sour Cream Dip

Makes: Eight servings
Prep Time: <10 minutes
Cook Time: 10 minutes or less, plus 1-hour chill time

This dip is a little spicy, a little tangy and addictive. Extremely simple to make, this will allow your guests to temper their taste buds to suit their own spice level preferences.

Ingredients

8 oz sour cream
OR 8 oz unflavored Greek yogurt
2 tsp whole black peppercorns, coarsely crushed
10 stems of fresh mint leaves (not peppermint)
3 jalapeños or Fresno peppers, deseeded
1 tsp fresh lemon juice
Salt, to taste

Method

Trim the fresh mint leaves; save the tips for garnish. Use an herb mill or a sharp knife to finely chop the mint leaves and jalapeños, taking care to ensure that the pieces are tiny. Transfer the sour cream (or yogurt) into a mixing bowl and add the mint leaves, jalapeños, crushed black pepper, lemon juice and salt. Combine well. Return this mixture to a serving bowl of your choice and decorate with the fresh mint leaves. Cover and chill for 1 hour or more before serving.

Phudina Dahi

Mint-Yogurt Dip

Makes: Eight servings
Prep Time: 15 minutes
Cook Time: 5 minutes plus 1 hour to chill

This simple dip complements most stuffed parathas. It is quick and easy, and can be prepared a day ahead.

Ingredients

1 cup fresh mint leaves
6 tsp fresh dill leaves
2 tsp nigella seeds
1″ fresh ginger
2 cups unflavored Greek yogurt
½ cup small curd cottage cheese (optional)
1 tsp salt
½ tsp sugar
2 tsp lime juice

Method

Trim the fresh mint leaves and dill leaves; save the tips for garnish. In a small food processor, combine the mint leaves, dill leaves, nigella seeds and ginger into a smooth paste. In a large mixing bowl, combine this paste with the yogurt and whisk until smooth. Add the small curd cottage cheese, salt, sugar and lime juice. Garnish with the reserved mint and dill leaves. Cover with plastic wrap and chill for 1 hour prior to serving.

God Dahi

Honey-Ginger Yogurt

Makes: Four servings
Prep Time: 5 minutes
Cook Time: Nil

This simple yogurt makes an excellent dipping accompaniment to Adai. It can also be made ahead.

Ingredients
16 oz unflavored Greek yogurt
2 tsp honey
½" fresh ginger, grated

Method
Combine honey and grated ginger with the yogurt. Stir and set aside to chill for 20 minutes before serving. Serve cold.

Beetroot Raita

Creamy Onion & Beetroot Salad

Makes: Eight servings
Prep Time: 20 minutes
Cook Time: 5-8 minutes

This is my take on an old-fashioned raita or yogurt-based salad. Filled with the goodness of beetroots, this makes for a wonderful addition to the plate.

Ingredients
2 tbsp ghee
1 tsp black mustard seeds
1 tsp cumin seeds
1 large white or yellow onion, slivered
1 tbsp ginger paste
1 fresh curry leaf frond, or about 20 individual leaves
1 large jalapeño, diced
1 large beetroot, see Pre-Prep note
½ tsp salt
½ tsp lemon juice
2 cups unflavored Greek yogurt

Pre-Prep
Rinse the beetroot and boil in water for 3-5 minutes until fork tender. Remove the water and allow the beetroot to cool. Beetroot stains are impossible to remove – use surfaces that can be cleaned immediately. Gloves are recommended. Gently peel away the skin of the beetroot and grate. Use a grater that will produce shreds that are as wide as, or slightly narrower than linguini; anything smaller will create a lumpy mess.

Method
In a medium saucepan, heat the ghee. Add the mustard seeds and cumin seeds, and allow these to pop and release their flavors. Add the slivered onions and sauté until they soften slightly. Add the ginger paste, curry leaves and jalapeño, and sauté. Add the shredded beetroot. Stir and cook for 1 minute. Season with salt and a dash of lemon juice. Remove from heat and cool completely. Just prior to serving, add in the yogurt and mix thoroughly. Enjoy cold.

Onion & Beetroot Raita

Dalimbi Koshimbir

Creamy Pomegranate, Scallion & Cucumber Salad

Makes: Twelve servings
Prep Time: 10 minutes
Cook Time: Nil

Another family favorite, this raita benefits from fresh ingredients and seasonal pomegranate.

Ingredients

2 cups unflavored Greek yogurt, whisked
1 bunch green onions or scallions, sliced, including greens
2 large salad cucumbers, diced
8 small red radishes, sliced (optional)
Salt, to taste
Whole black peppercorns, cracked, to taste
Pinch of nigella seeds for garnish
¼ cup pomegranate arils

Method

Trim the vegetables and set them aside.
In a large serving bowl, whisk the yogurt until smooth. Add the sliced green onions, diced cucumbers, sliced radishes, salt and cracked pepper, and stir well until combined. Set aside in the refrigerator for 5 minutes so that the flavors mix well. Garnish with sprinkling of nigella seeds and pomegranate arils just before serving.

Peru Chutney

Creamy Ripe Guava Salad

Makes: 1½ cup
Cook Time: 10 minutes

This chutney is a party hit and is unusual in that it uses a soft ripe guava to add an unexpected dimension to the preparation.

Ingredients

1 tbsp ghee
1 tsp brown cumin seeds
¼ tsp ginger paste
¼ tsp cayenne pepper powder
Flesh of 4 large soft over ripe guavas, see Pre-Prep note
¼ cup yogurt
¼ cup raw unsalted peanuts, lightly roasted, husked and crushed to a coarse powder
Salt, to taste
½ tsp sugar

Pre-Prep

Prepare the guavas just before beginning the cooking process as the guava flesh will oxidize. Cut the guava into wedges and coarsely mash them with a potato masher. Using either a food mill or a large sieve, push this pulp through to reduce or eliminate the seeds. Scoop out as much as you can into a container. Cover this pulp with a cling film until ready to use.

Method

Heat the ghee in a shallow saucepan, and add the cumin seeds and ginger paste. Allow this to cook for 1 minute until the ghee is fragrant. Add the cayenne pepper powder and remove from heat. When the spiced ghee has cooled, add the guava pulp, yogurt, and crushed peanuts. Add a pinch of salt to taste, and the sugar. Stir well and keep refrigerated until ready to use. Use within the hour.

Amb'ya Chi Koshimbir

Creamy Ripe Mango Raita

Makes: 1½ cup
Cook Time: 10 minutes + 30 minutes chill time

Another delicious fruit-based chutney that takes advantage of seasonally available soft ripe mangoes. Use ripe Kent or Champagne for a sweet raita, or Australian or Red Mangoes for a tangy one. This raita must be chilled before serving.

Ingredients

1 tbsp ghee
1 tsp mustard seeds
¼ tsp ginger paste
1 frond curry leaves
½ jalapeno, deseeded and sliced
Flesh of 1 large ripe mango, diced, see Pre-Prep note
¼ cup yogurt, gently whisked
Salt, to taste

Pre-Prep

Rinse and dry the mango fruit. Using a vegetable peeler, peel away the skin. Trim the fruit as you would a pitted fruit and dice the flesh into half-inch pieces. Cover with plastic wrap until ready to use.

Method

Heat the ghee in a shallow saucepan, and add the mustard seeds to this and allow them to pop. Add ginger paste, curry leaves, and jalapeno and sauté for about half minute. Mix in the diced mango flesh and coat it with the spices. Remove from the heat. Allow this to cool for 2-5 minutes. When the mix appears cool, add the yogurt and salt and combine well until the mango pieces are completely covered in the yogurt. Refrigerate for thirty minutes or more until ready to use.

Lasun Chi Chutney

Spicy Garlic Peanut Chutney

Makes: Two cups
Prep Time: <30 minutes
Cook Time: <15 minutes

This is the Indian version of pesto. A rather rustic preparation of garlic, peanuts and red chili peppers, it can be made a week in advance.

Ingredients

4 tbsp oil
1 tsp cumin seeds
1 tsp white sesame seeds
10-12 whole dried red chilies
1½ cups peeled garlic cloves
¼ cup raw unsalted peanuts, dry-roasted, and skinned
¼ cup fresh mint leaves or leaves from 10 stems
2 tbsp lemon juice
1 tsp salt

Method

Heat the oil in a large saucepan. When the oil is hot but not smoking, add cumin seeds. Turn the heat down completely and add sesame seeds. Stir constantly until the seeds are just a slight shade darker than before. Stir in the dried red chilies and whole garlic cloves. Increase the heat to medium-high and cook the garlic for 2-3 minutes. Stir constantly. Add the peanuts and cook for another 2 minutes. Finish by adding the lemon juice, mint leaves and salt, and remove from heat when the peanuts are just turning golden. Allow mixture to cool completely. Grind this mixture in a food processor to a coarse granular paste. It must not be as runny as fresh pesto. Transfer into a clean, dry, airtight glass jar and store in the refrigerator.

Thekkali Chutney

South Indian Styled Tomato Relish

Makes: Eight servings
Prep Time: 20 minutes
Cook Time: <20 minutes

A traditional pairing for dishes from Southern India, this travel-friendly treat also survives a few hours without refrigeration. So, pack it for your next picnic or a summer brunch.

Ingredients

2 tsp oil
1 tsp black mustard seeds
½ tsp fenugreek seeds
1 medium onion, finely diced
2-3 garlic cloves, minced
Leaflets from 2 curry leaf fronds
1-2 tsp cayenne pepper powder
1 cup fresh tomato puree OR 2 cups cherry tomatoes, halved
1 tbsp tamarind paste concentrate
1 tsp sugar
Salt, to taste
Fresh cilantro leaves for garnish

Method

Heat the oil in a heavy-bottom saucepan. Add the mustard and fenugreek seeds to the hot oil. As the mustard seeds begin to pop, add the diced onion and stir until soft and golden. Add the minced garlic and curry leaves, and stir. Cook this mixture for 1-2 minutes on medium-low until the garlic is cooked but not brown. Add the cayenne pepper powder and stir; follow up with tomato puree or halved cherry tomatoes and tamarind paste. Increase the heat to medium and bring to a boil, constantly stirring and allowing the water content to evaporate. Season with sugar and salt, and let it cool. Transfer to a glass container and store in the refrigerator until ready to use. Use a clean, dry spoon to extract only the amount you will use. Garnish with cilantro while serving. Refrigerated, this chutney keeps well for 3-4 days.

Pithla'

Chickpea Gravy

Makes: Four to six servings
Cook Time: 20 minutes

This is a traditional pairing with Ghadichya Poly'a from Western India. It comes together quickly and is a must-have dish for a regional feast.

Ingredients

1 tsp oil
1 tsp cumin seeds
1 tsp black mustard seeds
¼ cup finely chopped white onions
1 tsp fresh garlic paste (optional)
5-6 fresh curry leaves
1-2 jalapeños split lengthwise
¼ tsp hing (asafetida powder)
¼ tsp turmeric powder
1 cup chickpea flour, sifted
½ cup water, add extra as needed
½ cup unflavored Greek yogurt
Salt, to taste
Cilantro leaves from 4-5 stems, finely chopped (optional)

Method

Whisk the chickpea flour with water, yogurt, salt, and chopped cilantro leaves, set aside until ready to use. This mixture should not have any lumps.
Heat the oil in a small heavy-bottom saucepan. As it heats up, add the mustard seeds, cumin seeds and allow them to season the oil as the mustard seeds crack open. Add the onions, garlic paste, curry leaves and jalapeños (if using), cook to soften. Turn the heat down to low, add the turmeric powder and hing, and stir in to let it cook slightly. Do not let it burn. Immediately add the prepared chickpea sauce and stir vigorously. Continue stirring for 3-4 minutes until the gravy thickens and begins to leave the side of the pan. Add water to change the consistency of the gravy as desired. Garnish with chopped cilantro (if using). Serve hot over steamed rice or with pol'y.

Aloo Chaat Raita

Twice-cooked Creamy Potato Salad with Radish & Dill

Makes: Eight servings
Prep Time: 20 minutes
Cook Time: 5-8 minutes

This raita balances the sharp flavors of radish and red onions with the cooling flavors of yogurt and the simple red potato, and picks up the high notes from fresh dill for an elegant twist to a traditional favorite.

Ingredients

2 tbsp ghee
1 tsp black mustard seeds
1 large red onion, slivered
1 tbsp fresh ginger, julienned
2 cups diced red skin potatoes, boiled with skin on
2 cups unflavored Greek yogurt, whisked
5-8 red radishes cut into disks
Salt, to taste
1 tsp chaat masala (optional)
1 tsp fresh dill leaves

Method

Heat the ghee in a large saucepan. Add the mustard seeds and allow these to pop. Add the slivered onions and sauté until they soften slightly. Add the julienned ginger and sauté. Carefully add the boiled red-skin potatoes and cook them on medium low until the skins look crispy and the cubes begin to fry a little, 3-5 minutes. Once the potatoes have fried, remove from the heat in a bowl and allow to cool completely. Carefully add in the whisked yogurt, red radish disks, season with salt, chaat masala if using, and half of the fresh dill leaves. Mix gently to keep the potatoes from crumbling. Garnish with the remaining dill leaves, cover with plastic wrap and cool thoroughly before serving.

Aloo Choley Raita

Twice-cooked Creamy Potato Salad with Garbanzo Beans

Makes: Eight servings
Prep Time: 20 minutes
Cook Time: 5-8 minutes

This raita pairs seemingly plain ingredients into a flavorful side dish. It can be made up to 2 days ahead.

Ingredients

2 tbsp ghee
1 tsp black mustard seeds
1 large red onion, slivered
1 tbsp fresh ginger, julienned
1 can garbanzo beans, drained and rinsed
1 cup diced red skin potatoes, boiled with skin on
2 cups unflavored Greek yogurt, whisked
Salt, to taste
1 tsp fresh cilantro leaves (optional)

Method

Heat the ghee in a large saucepan. Add the mustard seeds and allow these to pop and release their flavors. Add the slivered onions and sauté until they soften slightly. Add the julienned ginger and sauté. Carefully add the drained garbanzo beans and diced potatoes, and let them cook on medium low until they take on some of the spices, 3-5 minutes. Remove the pan from the heat allow it to cool completely. Carefully add in the whisked yogurt and season with salt. Mix gently to keep the potatoes from crumbling. Garnish with the cilantro leaves, cover with plastic wrap and cool thoroughly before serving.

Aloo Choley Raita

Khattey Meethey Gajar

Sweet & Sour Fresh Carrot Salad

Makes: Eight servings
Cook Time: 15 minutes, plus 30 minutes or more to chill

Crunchy and good, this is one excellent way to add carrots to your lunch or dinner table. Loaded with tangy flavors, vitamins and a boost of fiber, this makes an ideal accompaniment to any meal.

Ingredients

1 tbsp butter/ghee
1 tsp ginger paste
1 tsp garlic paste
1 tsp fennel seeds
2 cups grated organic carrots
½ tsp orange zest
1 tsp julienned mint leaves
1 tsp sugar
Juice of ¼ orange
Pinch of salt
Dash of whole black peppercorns, cracked

Method

In a small saucepan, heat the butter or ghee until it melts. Add the fennel seeds and allow it to sizzle. When they become fragrant, add the ginger-garlic paste stir in, remove from heat and cool completely. In a large bowl, spread out the grated carrots. Sprinkle in a teaspoon of sugar. Pour the fennel seasoning into the carrots; add the orange zest, mint leaves, orange juice, salt and cracked pepper. Toss this mixture generously. Cover and chill for at least 1 hour before serving.

Teekha-Meetha Pineapple Raita

Sweet-n-Spicy Pineapple Salad

Makes: 1½ cup
Cook Time: 10 minutes + 30 minutes chill time

Another delicious fruit-based raita that is quick to assemble. Both canned and fresh pineapple work just as well for this dish. This raita must be chilled before serving.

Ingredients

1 tbsp ghee
1 tsp mustard seeds
¼ tsp ginger paste
1 frond curry leaves
½ jalapeno, deseeded and sliced
1 cup diced fresh pineapple OR
1 cup canned crushed pineapple, juices reserved
¼ cup yogurt, gently whisked
Salt, to taste

Method

Heat the ghee in a shallow sauce pan, and add the mustard seeds to this and allow them to pop. Add ginger paste, curry leaves, and jalapeno and sauté for half a minute. Mix in the pineapple and coat it with the spices. Remove from the heat. Allow this to cool for 2-5 minutes. When the mix appears cool, add the yogurt and salt and combine well until the mango pieces are completely covered in the yogurt. Refrigerate for at least half an hour before serving.

Khattey Meethay Gajar using a mix of grated orange and black carrots for a seasonal side dish.

Gol-Keri

Indian-styled Mango Salsa

Makes: One cup
Prep Time: 30 minutes
Cook Time: Nil

One of our favorite ways to eat tart mangoes in the summer is this salsa. Use mangoes that are not fibrous.

Ingredients

¼ cup finely diced red or white onions
¼ tsp salt
1 Australian mango, skin removed, diced
½ tsp cumin coriander powder
1 tsp cayenne pepper powder
4 tbsp finely grated jaggery
Salt, to taste

Method

Dust the onions with the salt and set aside for 15 minutes to let the onions sweat. Using a muslin cloth or strainer, extract and remove as much of the onion juice as possible. Rinse once after done and squeeze any remaining water away from the onions. Spread the onions onto a paper towel for 5 minutes.

Mix all remaining ingredients in a large bowl until well combined. Stir carefully to keep the mango pieces intact. Add the red onion and mix again. This salsa is best consumed cold, within 2 days of preparation.

Shaak-no Sambharo

Quick Pickled Vegetables

Makes: Four to six 6 oz. jars
Prep Time: 20 minutes
Cook Time: 15 minutes

Quick pickled vegetables are welcomed any time of the year. Use fresh produce like cauliflower, carrots, radish, radish pods or especially raw turmeric for this preparation. Unlike most other preparations, here, the spice mix is created first, and includes salt and the vegetables are added at the very end before the pickle is stored to ensure even distribution.

Ingredients

⅓ cup vegetable oil
4 tbsp black mustard seeds (or 4 tbsp of store-bought mustard halves)
3 tbsp fenugreek seeds (or 3 tbsp. of store-bought fenugreek halves)
1 tsp asafetida powder
1 tbsp cayenne pepper powder, to taste (optional), OR
1 large serrano pepper deseeded, and sliced thin,
⅓ cup ginger julienned, optional, see Pre-Prep note
2-4 tbsp vinegar
2 tsp salt (optional)
2 cups mixed vegetables, see Pre-Prep note

Pre-Prep

Trim fresh vegetables like cauliflower, carrots, radish and others into bite sized pieces, and no larger than the container they will be stored in. Flash steam vegetables like cauliflower and carrots, and lay them on a kitchen towel to dry. If using fresh turmeric, cover the chopping board in plastic wrap, and wear gloves. Scrape off the skin with a spoon as you would for ginger and rinse it clean to wash away any tough bits. Pat each fingerling down and slice into thin rounds or to match the ginger, and place on a paper towel to air dry. All vegetables must be dry to touch before pickling.

To prepare ginger, peel and slice ginger into eighth-inch-thick slices, and chop them to look like carrot sticks. Spread on a paper towel and set aside to air dry for 15-20 minutes.

If using whole mustard seeds or whole fenugreek seeds, in two separate sets, crush each in a spice mill in short bursts until they each are broken down but not powdered. They should be the consistency of coffee grounds.

Method

Heat the oil in a large, wide mouth saucepan until it is hot but not smoking. Reduce the heat to low. Slowly add all the spices: mustard halves, fenugreek halves, asafetida powder, cayenne pepper if using, along with the jalapeno if using and ginger sticks. Also add in the vinegar and salt at the same time. Allow this to sizzle for a minute on low. Stir to allow the heat to distribute evenly. When the oil is aromatic, slowly add the trimmed vegetables and stir it in well. Turn up the heat and let this cook for 4-5 minutes until vegetables appear to have absorbed the spices a little. Turn off the heat and cover with a paper towel to capture any steam. Allow this to come to room temperature before storing.

Shaak-no sambharo with carrots and red radishes. Add curry leaves, if available, for added flavor.

To Store

Use smaller (4 – 6 oz.) sanitized and dry glass jars to store the pickle. Using a clean and dry spoon that is smaller than the mouth of the jar, ladle out portions of the pickle into each jar. Don't worry if you don't get the oils or juices when first filling the jars. Fill jars at least a half inch below the rim of the jar. Shake them once to allow the pieces to settle. Divide up any of the liquid over each of these jars, taking care that each jar has some of the spicy sauce. Lightly shake each jar to ensure the liquid finds its way into the nooks and crannies of vegetable pieces. Close the lid and store in the fridge.

The pickle is ready to eat immediately after it is made, but the flavors are pronounced after a day or two. Serve using a clean and dry fork or spoon for each serving to avoid contamination.

Neembu Achar

Quick Pickled Keylimes

Makes: Four to six, 6 oz. jars
Prep Time: 20 minutes, plus drying time
Cook Time: 15 minutes, plus cooling time

When keylimes are plentiful, we make this pickle and make it often. It pairs well with most Indian meals and is a good standby if you are looking to perk up your plate.

Ingredients

4 lb key limes
⅔ cup mustard oil or vegetable oil
8 tbsp black mustard seeds
OR
4 tbsp of store-bought mustard halves
6 tbsp fenugreek seeds
OR
3 tbsp of store-bought fenugreek halves
2 tbsp cayenne pepper powder (to taste)
2 tsp asafetida powder
2-3 tbsp Lucknowi fennel seeds, whole (optional)
¼ cup julienned ginger (optional, see Pre-Prep note)
2 tsp salt (optional)

Pre-Prep

Wash the key limes and dry them with a clean dish towel. Spread them out to air dry thoroughly for 2-3 hours on a paper towel. Once completely dry, cut them into halves first and then cut each half into quarters and set aside in a bowl, juices and all.

If using whole mustard seeds or whole fenugreek seeds, in two separate sets, crush each in a spice mill in short bursts until they each are broken down but not powdered. They should be the consistency of coffee grounds.

If using ginger, spread the julienned ginger on a paper towel and aside to air dry for 15-20 minutes.

Method

Heat the oil in a large, wide mouth saucepan until it is hot but not smoking. Reduce the heat to low. Slowly add all the spices: mustard halves, fenugreek halves, cayenne pepper, asafetida powder and fennel seeds, as well as the ginger sticks, and salt if using. Allow this to sizzle for a minute on low. Stir to allow the heat to distribute evenly. When the oil is aromatic with all the spices, slowly add the cut key limes with its juices and all and stir it in well. Turn up the heat and let this cook for 4-5 minutes until the key limes appear to have softened just a little. The key limes will give off much of their juice into the oil and give it an opaque appearance. This is normal. Turn off the heat and cover with a paper towel. Allow this to come to room temperature before storing.

To Store

Use smaller (4 – 6 oz.) sanitized and dry glass jars to store the pickle. Using a clean and dry spoon that is smaller than the mouth of the jar, ladle out portions of the pickle into each jar. Don't worry if you don't get the oils or juices when first filling the jars. Fill jars atleast a half inch below the rim of the jar. Gently shake them once to allow the pieces to settle. Divide up any of the liquid over each of these jars, taking care that each jar has some of the spicy sauce. Lightly shake each jar to ensure the liquid finds its way into the nooks and crannies of the key lime pieces. Close the lid and store in the fridge.

The key lime pickle is ready to eat immediately after it is made, but the flavors are pronounced after a day or two. Serve using a clean and dry fork or spoon for each serving to avoid contamination.

Rasbhari Achaar

Calcutta-styled Golden Berry Pickle

Makes: Four to six, 6 oz. jars
Prep Time: 20 minutes, plus drying time
Cook Time: 15 minutes, plus cooling time

Golden berries are an unexpected treat in the grocery store. This quick pickle offers a nice way to bring it into your culinary repertoire.

Ingredients

¼ cup vegetable oil
2 tsp nigella seeds
2 tsp white poppy seeds
2 tsp whole black peppercorns, coarsely crushed
2 tsp Lucknowi fennel seeds, whole
1 frond curry leaves (optional)
4 cups husked and washed golden berries, halved
2 tsp salt (optional)
2 tbsp lemon juice
1 tsp sugar

Method

Heat the oil in a large, wide mouth saucepan until it is hot but not smoking. Reduce the heat to low. Slowly add all the spices: nigella seeds, poppy seeds, black peppercorns, fennel seeds, and curry leaves if using. Stir this well until all the spices are aromatic. Allow this to sizzle for a minute on low. Stir to allow the heat to distribute evenly and add the golden berries. Add the salt, lemon juice and sugar and sauté on low until they appear to soften, 2 minutes. Turn off the heat and cover with a paper towel. Allow this to come to room temperature before storing.

To Store

Transfer to sanitized and dry glass jars. Using a clean and dry spoon that is smaller than the mouth of the jar, ladle out portions of the pickle into each jar. The pickle is ready to eat immediately after it is made, and can be stored for up to a week in the refrigerator.

Methkut

Mixed Lentil Powder

Makes: 1¾ cup
Prep Time: 10 minutes plus dry time
Cook Time: 30 minutes

Popular all across Western India as a dipping powder for sides, add a tablespoon or two of Methkut to a bowl of Greek yogurt for a delicious dipping sauce for crunchy salad vegetables.

Ingredients

1 cup split, skinless channa daal
½ cup raw rice
¼ cup split yellow mung beans
2 tsp fenugreek seeds
4-5 whole red chilies, deseeded
1 tsp asafetida powder
¼ tsp cumin seeds

Method

Rinse all the channa daal, rice and split yellow mung beans. Allow them to dry on a tea towel for 2-3 hours, or overnight. Dry roast these the following day and set aside to air dry on a fresh tea towel. Dry roast each of these separately: fenugreek seeds, red chilies and cumin seeds. Combine all the roasted and unroasted ingredients, and grind to a fine powder. Sieve in between grinds to ensure a uniformly mixed powder. Serve a teaspoon of methkut with a dollop of warm home-made ghee.

Podi

Chutney Powder

Makes: Half cup
Prep Time: 10 minutes plus dry time
Cook Time: 10 minutes

A pantry staple in many households across Southern India, this podi or chutney powder offers a reliable dipping sauce or powder for many south Indian preparations as well as a mix for salad dressings (as paired with Paserattu). This powder stores well.

Ingredients

¼ cup skinless urad daal, see Pre-Prep note
¼ cup channa daal, see Pre-Prep note
1 tbsp oil
1 tsp mustard seeds
3-5 curry leaves
2 whole red chilies, deseeded
1 tsp turmeric powder
¼ tsp asafetida
2-4 tbsp toasted white sesame seeds (optional)
1 tsp salt

Pre-Prep

Rinse the skinless urad daal and the channa daal separately, drain and set aside on a shallow cookie sheet lined with paper towels. Let this dry completely before using.

Method

Toast the dried daals in a dry saucepan until they are lightly golden. Set aside on a cookie sheet lined with a paper towel.

Heat the oil in a saucepan on medium low, add the mustard seeds and curry leaves and allow this to season the oil for a minute. Add the seeded red chilies and toss to coat it in oil. Add the turmeric powder, asafetida and toasted sesame seeds, if using and mix in, Remove from heat. Add in the salt and the dried and roasted daals while the oil is still a little warm. When the entire mixture has cooled down completely, grind it in a spice mill into a fine powder. Store in a dry airtight container.

To Use: As Dipping Sauce Or Salad Dressing

Mix equal parts of podi with just warm cooking oil or ghee to make a creamy paste for dipping vegetable. If using as a salad dressing, blend in a teaspoon of podi with two to three teaspoons of warm olive oil and shake vigorously in a sealed jar. Drizzle over desired salad.

Shrikhand

Saffron Hung Yogurt

Makes: Eight servings
Cook Time: 5 minutes, plus 30 minutes or more to cool

This is a deliciously simple and tasty addition to any meal. The traditional method uses drained, hung yogurt that has little or no whey. Greek yogurt mimics the creamy texture without the effort.

Ingredients

Pinch of saffron, 6-8 strands
2 tbsp warm whole milk
32 oz unflavored full-fat Greek yogurt
½ cup sugar, to taste
2-3 green cardamom pods
¼ cup slivered almonds (optional)

Method

Soak the saffron in warm milk and set aside for a few minutes until the milk takes on a golden orange hue. Open the green cardamom pods and crush the black seeds until they are a fine powder. Transfer the yogurt into a large mixing bowl and whisk with an electric whisk until smooth. Add the sugar and whisk until fully combined. Check for sweetness, and adjust if necessary. Add the dissolved saffron, green cardamom powder and slivered almonds if using. Mix well with a large spoon and transfer to a glass bowl. Cover with plastic wrap, and refrigerate for half an hour or more until chilled. Serve cold.

Adrakwala Ananas Shrikhand

Pineapple & Ginger Hung Yogurt

Makes: Eight servings
Cook Time: 5 minutes, plus 30 minutes or more to cool

A variation on the classic shrikhand, this one pairs fruits and candied ginger for those who want more complex desserts. Although cardamom enhances the flavors, it is an optional ingredient in this dish.

Ingredients

Pinch of saffron, 6-8 strands
2 tbsp warm whole milk
32 oz unflavored whole milk Greek yogurt
2-3 green cardamom pods (optional)
½ can of pineapple bits, juices included
10-12 large pieces of candied ginger, cut into slivers

Method

Soak the saffron in warm milk and set aside for a few minutes until the milk takes on a golden orange hue. Open the green cardamom pods and crush the black seeds until they are a fine powder. Transfer the yogurt into a large mixing bowl and whisk with an electric whisk until smooth. Using a spatula, fold in the pineapple bits with its juices, the dissolved saffron, green cardamom powder and half of the candied ginger. Mix well with a large spoon and transfer to a glass bowl, garnish with the remaining candied ginger. Cover with plastic wrap, and refrigerate for half an hour or more until chilled. Serve cold.

Pineapple & ginger hung yogurt

Fruit Salaad

Mixed Fruit with Custard

Makes: Eight servings
Cook Time: 15 minutes, plus 30 minutes or more to cool

A classic dessert in India made with a particular brand of "custard powder," this recipe easily mimics the flavors without a trip to the ethnic store. Custard can be made ahead and chilled up to 2 days ahead of time. Pair it with seasonal fruit or a selection of mixed fruits like apples, grapes, peeled orange segments, bananas, strawberries, pomegranate etc. Unlike a tossed vegetable salad, the inclusion of fruits in a slightly runny eggless custard makes this a 'Fruit Salaad.'

Ingredients

4 cups plus 3 tbsp whole milk
½ cup sugar, to taste
2 tsp vanilla extract
3 tbsp corn starch
2-3 cups mixed fresh fruit, trimmed into bite sized pieces

Method

In a small bowl, mix the 3 tbsp room temperature whole milk with the corn starch and stir well until dissolved and set aside. Bring 4 cups of whole milk to a low simmer in a heavy bottom saucepan. Stir as it warms through to avoid burning at the bottom. As it comes to a boil, turn down the heat, add the sugar and stir again for another 5 minutes on low until small foam-like bubbles form at the edge. Add the vanilla extract and the corn starch mixed in with milk. Bring the milk to a boil again and check for sweetness. Keep stirring until the mixture thickens. Remove from heat and set it to cool for 10 minutes until the custard stops steaming. Place the saucepan in a cold ice bath to thicken the custard more. When it has completely cooled, transfer to a glass container and chill for half an hour until ready to use.

To Serve

There are many ways to serve this custard. These are the two most popular ones, either pour the chilled custard over individual servings of fruit in a bowl, or mix the fruit into the custard and ladle out individual servings. Serve cold.

One Last Bite

As this book showcases, breads in the Indian cuisine are individually crafted, lovingly cooked and reflect the patience and care of the person who made them. With each meal, one sees how health and nutrition merge into one "dish." Whole grains and seasonal produce are easily incorporated into many preparations, improving nutrient content. Even root vegetables, squashes, and leafy greens make an appearance, further enhancing the health benefits of a made-from-scratch meal. India's bread offerings extend far beyond restaurant selections of naan, parathas or makai-ki-roti, and of course, offers many alternatives to experiment with. This book deliberately chose simple recipes, showcasing the many varieties of bread that are consumed every single day across a large subcontinent. They are prepared by homemakers every single day, without fancy tools or equipment – in the most basic ways possible.

There is a resurgence of interest in local ancient grains like fox-grain millets, barnyard millets, amaranth, proso millet, kodo millet, and others, and it would be wonderful to know how to cook with them in our present-day kitchens. A countertop flour mill may be in order to convert these into flour to retain their nutrients. Once mastered, look for dishes unique to the many gastronomic regions of India: dhebra, a variation of Thepla from western state of Gujarat, Sheermal – a saffron bread popular in the mountains of Northern India, Roomali Roti – a muslin thin sheet of stretched dough, varieties of laminated pastries called "Puffs" stuffed with tangy and delicious fillings, Kulcha, Tandoori Rotis, Laccha Paratha, Malabari Paratha, Litti and Baati: coal-roasted croquette stuffed with regional specialties from the North and North-western India, and many others. I hope that by the time you have become comfortable with the techniques in this book, we will have another edition of Roti with these and other kinds of bread from even more kitchens across India, and also pickles, chutneys and relishes that have delighted the masses for centuries.

APPENDIX

Multipurpose Visual Guides

Dough for roti/rotli, paratha, stuffed paratha etc

How to roll roti/rotli, fulka, paratha, etc

Cooking fulka rotli over open flame

Preparing & cooking a stuffed paratha, for instance "Gul poli"

Homestyle dosa & homestyle dosa with egg

Steps: Dough for roti/rotli, paratha, stuffed paratha etc

1. Assemble ingredients: flour, water, salt & oil.

2. Add salt.

3. Add half the water.

4. Reserve other half of the water for later.

5. Mix in the water with the flour.

6. Knead in all the dry flour.

7. Mix in the remaining water and knead again.

8. Add the oil and knead it in.

9. Finished ball of dough.

10. Divide the dough into equal portions for use.

Steps: How to roll roti/rotli, fulka, paratha, etc

1. Arrange workspace.

2. Dredge a single dough ball in dry flour.

3. Dust off excess dry flour.

4. Use pinched hold & light pressure.

5. Continue rolling, use 'pinched' hold.

6. Dust with dry flour as needed.

7. Spread dry flour, flip, continue rolling.

8. Finished, rolled uncooked roti.

1. Place rolled roti on warm non-stick griddle.

2. Cook on medium low until underside bubbles, the side touching the griddle is side #1.

3. Move it around once or twice, and flip it. Side #1 will be lightly spotted.

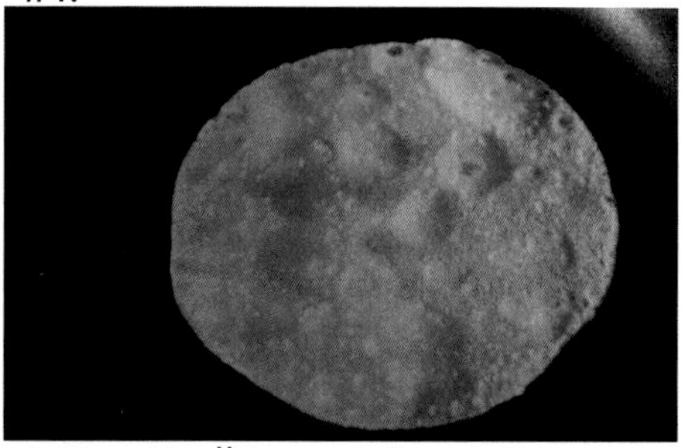

4. Allow side #2 to cook in a similar manner.

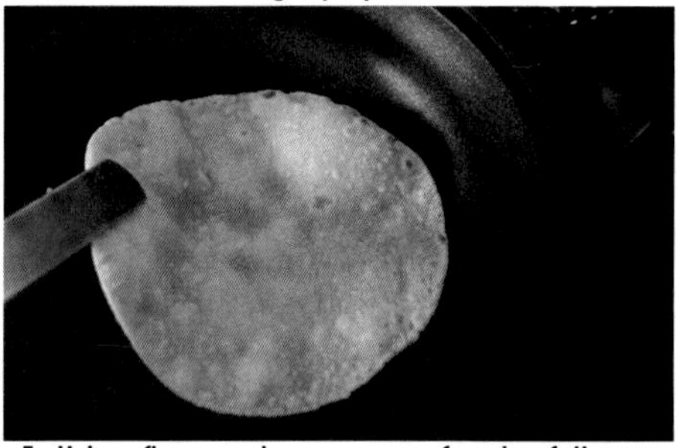

5. Using flat-nosed tongs, transfer the fulka onto the open flame.

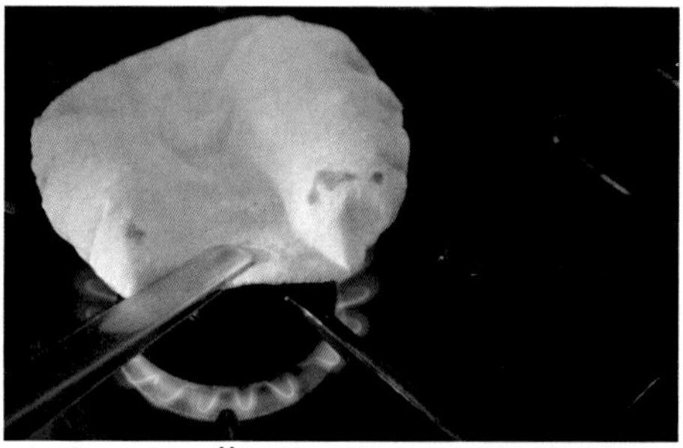

6. Place side #1 down onto the open flame.

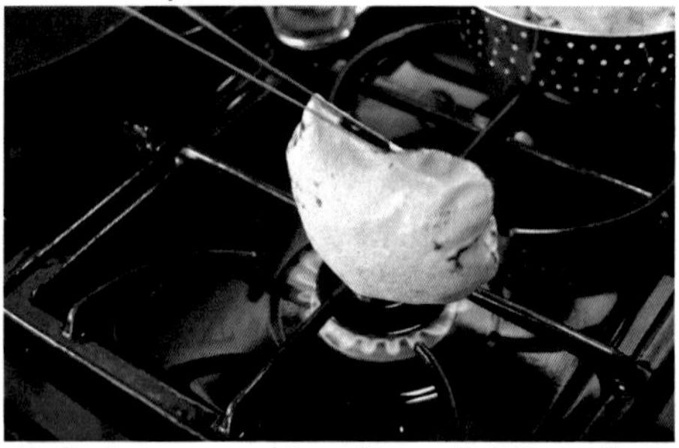

7. Cook once on either side until fulka puffs up, 7-10 seconds on each side.

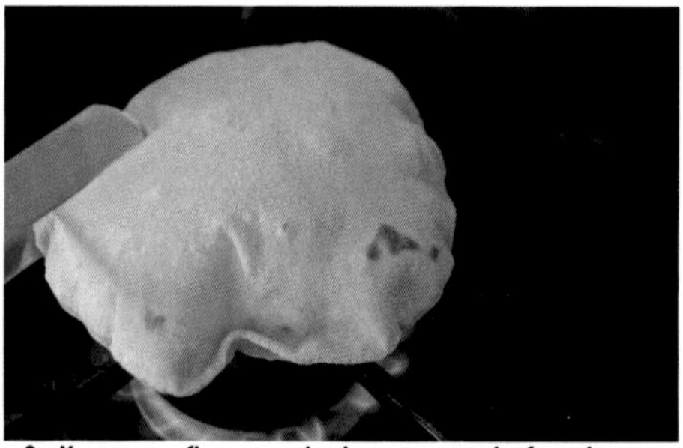

8. Keep on flame only long enough for the fulka to puff up, no more than twice on each side.

9. Remove from flame into a flat bottom colander.

10. Baste with melted ghee while it is still warm.

Steps: Preparing & cooking a stuffed paratha. for example, Gul Poli

1. Pour batter.

2. Spread batter.

3. Drizzle oil/ghee.

4. Flip.

5. Homestyle dosa.

Steps: Homestyle Dosa & Homestyle Dosa with Egg

Homestyle Dosa with Egg

4. Pour cracked egg.

5. Season, cover & cook in steam.

6. Homestyle dosa with egg.

Intuitive Guide

Special Diets

Wheat based

Gluten-free

On The Side

Savory Sides

Aloo Chaat Raita	112
Aloo Choley Raita	112
Amb'ya Chi Koshimbir	108
Cranberry Chutney	100
Dahi Chataka	103
Dalimbi Koshimbir	106
Kairywali Naralchi Chutney	98
Kakdi Koshimbir	102
Lasun Chi Chutney	109
Methkut	124
Neembu Achar	120
Peru Chutney	107
Phudina Dahi	103
Pithla'	111
Podi	125
Rasbhari Achaar	122
Shaak-no Sambharo	118
Thekkali Chutney	110

Sweet(er) Sides

Adrakwala Ananas Shrikhand	126
Beetroot Raita	104
Fruit Salaad	128
God Dahi	104
Gol-Keri	116
Khattey Meethey Gajar	114
Masala Cha	96
Shrikhand	126
Teekha Meetha Pineapple Raita	114

Desserts

Aapam / Hopper	90
Adrakwala Ananas Shrikhand	126
Bread Pudding	71
Fruit Salaad	128
Gul God Bhopla Poori	56
Kheer Patishapta	92
Malpua	89
Puran Poli	42
Shrikhand	126

Time-crunch

Bread-maker shortcuts {dough only}

Sleep-over-it {fermentation}

Timesavers: breads with make-ahead components

Timesavers: make-ahead sides

Short Glossary of Terms

Bhakri: a gluten-free griddle-fried bread.
Bread: unless otherwise specified, for the purposes of this book – the term refers to a meal component and not the preparation itself.
Chutney: a pesto-like, pasty preparation, that is typically dairy-free.
Dosa: a crepe-like preparation from Southern India but can also be a generic term for a thin soft crepe.
Koshimbir: a regional term for a side made with a selection of vegetables, dressed with a plain whisked yogurt.
Paratha: a griddle fried bread that may or may not be stuffed.
Pickle: a generic term for a side that includes vegetables that are flash pickled or marinated over time in spices and oil. Its shelf life varies by preparation.
Poori: a generic term for a fried bread. Size, composition and flavor varies by region.
Poora: a generic term for a savory pancake like bread, typically made with chickpea flour.
Raita: a generic term for a side dressed with tempered yogurt.
Roti/rotli/fulka/phulka/chapati: regional though generic terms for a wheat-based flat bread that is lightly basted with butter, ghee or oil.
Salad: a generic term for a mélange of finely chopped raw vegetables treated as a side. This is typically not dressed.

Select Reading

Achaya, K. T., Indian Food: A Historical Companion, Oxford India Paperbacks, 1998

Ammal, S. Meenakshi, The Best Of Samaithu Paar, Penguin Random House India, 2018

Batra, Neelam, Rothschild, Shelly Sherwin, The Indian Vegetarian: Flavors For The American Kitchen, MacMillan, 1994

Iyer, Raghavan 660 Curries, Workman Publishing, 2016

Jaffrey, Madhur, Invitation to Indian Cooking, Knoff, 2011

Marks, Copeland, The Varied Kitchens of India: Cuisines of the Anglo-Indians of Calcutta, Bengalis, Jews of Calcutta, Kashmiris, Parsis, and Tibetans of Darjeeling Cuisines of the Anglo-Indians of Calcutta, Bengalis, Jews of Calcutta, Kashmiris, Parsis and Tibetans of Darjeeling, M. Evans n Company, 1991

Marks, Gil, Encyclopedia of Jewish Food, Houghton Mifflin Harcourt, 2010

INDEX

D

E

F

R

S

T

U

V

W

Y

Z

About the author

Nandita is an Atlanta based, Indian origin author. Her work has found mention in Forbes, NBC, NBC-Asian America, Publishers' Weekly and many others. Her global reach in readership is on account of her pragmatic approach to cooking, and therefore appealing to all levels of culinary enthusiasts. As a food writer and a cultural observer, her essays appear periodically in digital and print media where she shares perspectives on a wide range of topics. She loves to travel to food destinations, always seeking out the flavor, and everyday culture, because they represent the essence of life. Read more about her, her work, and her thinking at currycravings.com and currycravingskitchen.com, or follow along on social media @currycravings.

• Other Titles by Author

Ten Thousand Tongues: secrets of a layered kitchen, foreword by Neela Paniz, 2018
Ten Thousand Tongues: the companion cookbook, 2018
Crack The Code: Cook Any Indian Meal With Confidence, foreword by Faye Levy, Second Edition, 2016
A Dozen Ways to Celebrate: Twelve Decadent Indian Feasts for the Culinary Indulgent, 2014